Context Is Everything

Context Is Everything

How to Navigate Life in
Multiple Realities

David James Bright

Contents

chapter one

It Began on an Island

The idea for this book dawned on me while I was on my honeymoon in Marco Island, Florida. Admittedly, plotting out a book probably wasn't the best use of my mental energy at the time. With endless sunshine and pristine gulf coast beaches, I should have been relaxing and soaking in every enjoyable moment with my wife. Still, as I sat on a chair and stared out a window (the glow of the sun and the soft lapping of the turquoise water tempting me to go on another beach walk), an intriguing thought came to mind.

My wife and I were staying at a high-end beach resort, the glitz, glamor, and quality higher than anything I could have ever imagined. I was born into generational poverty, raised in a true middle-of-nowhere rural area, and only a few years prior had taken my first professional job in Vermont. I'd driven to my new home with eighty dollars in my bank account and an air mattress in the back seat. That major leap was the beginning of the journey that had led me to this point. And where was I now?

Out of place, perhaps? No, that wasn't quite right, but the people spending time at this resort seemed to come from backgrounds I had rarely encountered and barely understood. My wife and I could only afford this exclusive retreat due to her saving up years' worth of hotel points. She traveled frequently for work and had strategized this long before our wedding details were set. I reflected on how I ended up in this position.

It felt surreal, as if it were a dream. After a life marred by tragedy, instability, and periods of depression, how could I end up here?

How could two seemingly separate worlds merge into one?

As I pondered this, I noticed a child. My observation was the type that often leaves as quickly as it comes, a blip on the radar so small it isn't even noted. This time, however, the backdrop of my reflective thoughts provided the perfect adhesive for it to stick. I observed a young boy, perhaps seven years of age, hopping up and down trying to get the attention of his parents, who were lounged back in their chairs outside, each enjoying an early-morning cocktail.

I thought how bizarre this resort must seem for children. Here were adults wasting their time sitting around, drinking, some of the single adults flirting at tiki bars, all of their time spent on leisure, when there was just so much fun to be had. There were multiple pools, an arcade, an entire ocean to play in—and here were these adults, adhering to strange social conventions, floating around in a constant semi-buzzed state, caught up in things that didn't matter.

I smiled, reflecting on the way I thought of adults when I was a kid. I remember how I thought they missed opportunities, prioritized the mundane, and stressed over the trivial. Then I flipped the switch, thinking about how children must appear to the adults on the resort. Hyper, overly emotional, unobservant, and unaware of economic realities. There were undoubtedly countless moments when the parents were left shaking their heads at the behavior and outlook of their children. It's just how parenting goes.

This is when the thought for the book hit me.

Here were two groups of people, in an objective sense experiencing the exact same environment and situation, coming away with thoughts and impressions that were completely different. What was causing such a different interpretation of the resort and each other? As a counselor by training, I felt it came down to one answer.

Context is everything.

As a child, I agreed with those kids who rolled their eyes at the adults relaxing for another five minutes before getting to the next activity. As an adult, I understand the necessity of downtime, relaxation, and the occasional early-morning cocktail. I am the same person, but the reality of my life situation, my experiences, my *context* is radically different.

I've earned a PhD in counselor education, and I work as an assistant professor of counseling. I've previously worked as a school, career, and mental health counselor across several institutions. I'm constantly interacting with individual context. The root of my job is to understand the wants, needs, environment, and worldview of individuals to help them process, grow, and find solutions. I've learned the value and power of context through these experiences, as well as just how prevalent it is in every interaction in our lives.

This book will be informed by a counseling perspective and by research in the field. These provide evidence-based backing to some of my thoughts and perspectives on context and on how, by better understanding and identifying these things, we all can live happier, healthier lives. But this is not an academic book destined to be riddled with jargon. Instead, I'm using my training, education, and experiences to provide insight and tangible action steps for just about everyone.

I will use plenty of real-world examples, modifying identifiers of the individuals to protect confidentiality. We will actually begin with a story, one that I've utilized with students to exemplify what I mean when I talk about the nature of context and the validity of individual realities.

I was working as a school counselor in a school in rural New Hampshire. It was a place where history had a different meaning, a *deeper* meaning, as just about every family in the district could trace their family lineage through the squat, boxy school building—the entire structure the size of a cafeteria in a large urban school. The building sat on a dirt road, adjacent to farmland, just a speck beneath the watchful gaze of the mountains, with natural beauty encompassing this relic and symbol of the community.

I was the first school counselor they'd had in five years. This elementary school had a population of about 115 students. Despite the limited number of students, needs were high, with approximately 75% of the students qualifying for free or reduced lunch, 50% having an academic or emotional support plan requiring some type of counseling, and in my estimation, about 40% of students having experienced some form of severe trauma. These figures changed the reality of that school. They altered the context, which then modified the nature of my job and how I responded to student needs. This all came together on the day in which I helped Anna.

Anna was a student in one of our lower grades. She'd had a difficult history, experiencing past trauma, neglect, and severe abuse, which all impacted her daily emotions and general functioning in school. While she was bright and cheery on a good day, her smile, charm, and sense of humor would disappear in an instant given the right trigger.

I was called into her classroom one day to assist with a situation. I walked in to see the teacher, who was a strong professional and cared about her students, in a confrontation with Anna, who was hiding under a table in a corner. Anna was crying and would respond to her teacher only by shouting, "No!" or letting out a piercing shriek. The teacher repeatedly said that if this behavior continued, there would be consequences, as per the class rules. The teacher was calm but clearly becoming exasperated, as she'd been trying to reach Anna for about ten minutes prior to me arriving. The teacher explained that she had simply reminded Anna of a class rule. When corrected, Anna became hostile and defensive, causing the teacher to ask Anna to take a time out. Upon this reprimand, Anna had an emotional meltdown, screaming, crying, and hiding in the corner. The teacher had relied on social structure and rules to try to reach Anna. If Anna would not come out, she would have to visit the principal and her mother would have to be called. I assured the teacher she could tend to the rest of her students while I worked with Anna.

What was going on here?

The teacher had given a student a simple reminder. Why, then, had the student reacted so strongly? Why was this young girl in such a state? Was it a bad attitude? A problem with authority? A lack of respect for rules?

I crawled on the floor over to Anna. She peeked out at me, a cursory glance, before quickly darting her gaze away. She sniffled and sobbed, hyperventilating and spitting up phlegm. Her focus wasn't on my presence, but on her own needs and state. She needed an escape in every sense of the word. I chose my first words to her very wisely, knowing it was my only hope of meeting her where she was at and helping her in that moment.

"You seem like you're really scared."

Anna peeked at me again, her gaze laden with curiosity instead of mistrust. She nodded before looking away, tucking her head back into the corner, and continuing sobbing. This was important, as I was no longer a foreign, invasive presence. I'd reached her, if ever so slightly.

"You seem like you're really scared," I repeated softly. "Is there anything I can do to help you?"

Anna shifted, regaining some of her composure. Her rate of breathing decreased and her body relaxed. After a minute of silence, she turned and faced me, expression neutral. She wasn't quite at the point of trust, but she was willing to speak.

"You're safe," I said. "But I know it's tough crying when all of your friends are around. Would you like to come to my office? We can play card games if you'd like."

Anna looked around as if appraising the danger of the situation, and then wiped her tears away. She quickly nodded and reached out for my hand. I took it, helping her to her feet and walking her to my office. There, we played card games and chatted casually until she was calm, at which point we could access her rational thought patterns and talk about what had happened. We then explored why it had happened and planned for how to avoid it next time.

Why did I take this approach?

Because the teacher and Anna were operating in different realities.

For the teacher, this was a small conflict, a simple correction. It was a common occurrence, and how she'd interacted with Anna was routine, nothing to be noted. To Anna, this was something much, much different.

Anna had experienced multiple severe traumas in her life. In her life experience, fight-or-flight-style reactions were *useful* in avoiding additional abuse. Tantrums were ways to avoid pain or even to get attention when facing neglect. Her mind didn't react to varying levels of stress differently, because it *couldn't afford to*; reacting with fight-or-flight was a necessary *survival* mechanism. Appraising and thinking through how to act can be a *detriment* when your safety and psychological well-being are *constantly being threatened*. When adults were upset with Anna, she had experienced abuse, so her mind and body reacted as if this were expected to come.

In fact, research shows that trauma has a *physical* impact on the development of the brain, literally stunting its growth and reducing the capability for higher-level functioning. Repeated trauma rewires the brain to respond according to an abusive situation and context— programming that often comes in conflict with the workings of the rest of the world. From birth to age 5, we are rapidly developing our brains, hardwiring the concepts of who we are, how we should act, and how to deal with danger.

So, what was *actually* happening here? Was the teacher doing her job properly, or was she an antagonistic threat to Anna? If you asked the teacher and most of the students, they'd likely say Anna was the one who was antagonistic, who was rude and disruptive, and who had caused the problem. If you asked Anna, she would honestly report to you that she was scared of the teacher and that in that moment she felt that everyone hated her and wanted to hurt her.

Both of these things were happening. Both of these things were real. If they had not been real, Anna would not have acted in the manner in which she did. Her legitimate fear and biochemical response compelled her to act as if her life was in danger. This *cannot* be ignored if we want to connect with and help Anna succeed in the classroom and foster positive peer relationships.

I couldn't reach Anna in a reality she couldn't access or understand. If I was to reach and help Anna, I had to meet her in her own reality. I had to treat the fear as real and respond in a way that showed I recognized it and cared for her safety.

Now, just because her feelings and reactions were real, this doesn't necessarily make them valid or appropriate for the situation. Anna's reaction was far beyond what was necessary for a simple correction. The teacher had been calm and had acted as she would with any student. But if Anna is reacting in a way that is not helpful in the situation, how should we approach her?

Any attempt to force Anna into the teacher's reality of rationality, rules, and consequences would only further embed Anna in her own perception. A stern tone, threats, punishment—all of these confirm to her that the teacher hates her and wants to hurt her, either physically or emotionally. This is Anna's frame for herself and the world: her experience taught her that adults wanted to hurt her, and if the teacher progressed by becoming more forceful, she would have proven Anna correct in her own mind. And truly, if this cycle continued for months every time Anna misbehaved, I'm sure the teacher would grow to resent Anna in some way. If our class were consistently derailed by a single student, wouldn't most of us become exasperated?

Trauma can cause a cycle to begin in a child where the negative interactions they experience as a result of their responses become confirmation that they are bad, wrong, hated, and unable to have healthy relationships. The world isn't a place that offers kindness, care, support, or understanding; it instead others them. Therefore, why try at school? Why try to develop positive relationships when they are destined to fade? Why trust others when this has only resulted in pain? Lashing out at others and developing negative coping habits makes a lot of sense given this framework. Many who struggle with trauma and coexisting conditions, such as drug addiction, are trying to avoid the wounds inflicted in their childhood, when love, security, and acceptance weren't provided. The wounds prevented them from finding this in others in their lives, and thus avoidant coping strategies are desired.

Anna was worthy of compassion and care. I had to provide it through meeting her where she was at. Her heart was beating out of her chest, her adrenaline was rapidly flowing, and her thoughts were racing at a rate faster than she could process. My response was not that she was breaking the rules or causing a problem. Instead, I responded in a caring way that emphasized concern for her safety. If Anna were feeling safe, secure, and cared about, she would not be acting in the manner in which she did.

I showed Anna that she was safe. I played games with her, shared jokes, and talked about what she wanted to talk about. I offered empathic statements about how hard the situation must have been for her. After she was calm, Anna admitted that she didn't have a good reaction to the situation. She realized the teacher was just enforcing the classroom rules, which she knew were important. Anna stressed that sometimes it became so hard to deal with her "big feelings." I made sure to let her know that even I had problems with "big feelings" all the time and that this was normal. Anna became open to working with me on controlling her thoughts and reactions and building a positive view of self and others. Although this meeting didn't immediately solve her challenges, it began a journey that ended a year later with her being one of the stars of the class and school.

When realities come into conflict, the solutions are not easy. Rather than modify instruction or come up with individual behavior plans, many schools prefer to take the one-size-fits-all approach. Trauma-informed care takes time and energy up front ... but most don't realize the immense benefits that come on the back end, not only benefiting in time but in the emotional wellness and overall success of children. In the short-term, many see it as easier to impose the rules, the "reality" of school, instead of understanding and adapting to work with the multiple lived realities of students. While it is difficult to adapt, as in Anna's case and that of countless others, it is effective and ends up with the best results for all. When we acknowledge and validate where people are at and why, they are *much more likely to have buy-in to what is being said and done.*

And that is what this book is about: adapting and navigating through conflicting realities. There will be counseling as well as other real-life examples of how we run into these things every day of our lives. A large chunk of this approach and philosophy is embedded in the concept of social constructivism. Like with the counseling and research data, I won't belabor the history and nuances of this philosophy, or its counterpart, objectivism; a brief explanation will suffice.

Social constructivists claim that there is no true singular reality. Rather, reality is constructed through individual and social interpretation. For example, the concept of justice is socially constructed—we have an idea of what this is due to how our society molds and creates the law. Justice isn't an essence in the world but is a human concept we all interpret and interact with differently. This is why different states and nations have different opinions of justice and methods of carrying it out—it's an ever-changing concept dependent on social opinion and culture.

Objectivism claims there are objective truths grounded in reality. There is definable justice regardless of individual interpretation. Although interpretations may differ, some interpretations are *right* and others are *wrong*, because some have a clearer understanding of true justice than others. These philosophies have existed and been used in schools of thought for going on thousands of years. In this book, I won't settle the ultimate reality question of constructivism versus objectivism, but I will take one stance.

Regardless of the nature of reality, people operate within socially constructed perspectives. Their individual reality, experience, and context dictate how they interact with the world, even in the face of objective facts. Objective facts and realities have different meanings and value to the individual based on their context and identity; thus, when we are dealing and interacting with a human being, we are interacting with someone operating in a socially constructed modality.

Take Anna, for example. Hitting her with objective facts of the situation was not effective in her socially constructed world. These "facts" did not resonate with her lived experience and the reality of her emotional state. You'll notice that this is how much of the world operates. Have you ever seen a social media argument where people throw "facts" at each other? The objective truth and realities are there, yet these devolve into name-calling shouting matches. It's almost as if the facts of the situation are less important to people than their subjective interpretation and framing of what these facts really mean.

So, while we can always argue about what is really happening and what is really there, this book more so focuses on *what's actually going on in our heads and in those of people all around us.* We encounter

countless differing and shifting social realities every day, and understanding what is going on, why it is happening, and what we can do
to grow, progress, and come together as people, is key. This book is
informed and inspired by my personal life, clinical work, research,
and teaching in a graduate program. I invite you to draw from your
own perspectives and life experiences as we explore our contexts and
those of the world around us.

chapter two

What Is Context?

I've already used the word *context* more times than some of you can bear. I'm sorry to say that its usage will continue throughout this book. But if I'm going to drone on about context and identity, I'd best describe exactly what I mean by these things. I could hit you with the definition, some social-ecological theory, perhaps, but I think it's best to start with an example of individual context and identity. And whose context and identity could I better speak to than my own?

I mentioned earlier that I was born into a family who experienced generational poverty. I bring this up because it is one of the foundations of my context. Growing up without much money fundamentally shaped how I look at myself and the world. Now, many of us look at this as a foregone conclusion. "Of course," I can practically hear you say, but what we often fail to consider is just how integral so many details of our childhood are to us forming the foundation of who we are.

What we believe the world is and should be is hardwired deeply into us during our formative years. We begin making connections by understanding the self as it relates to our own identity, to others, and to society. This is the structure and security of the world—how things are or should be. This is why we have generational trends and preferences, particularly within entertainment. This is seen in the idea of "good music" or "quality television shows." It's all preference, but this preference is often founded in the sociocultural experiences of our youth.

The problem is, we tend to treat these outlooks and opinions as facts. We aren't exactly biologically designed for nuance. In fact, our minds react in a similar way to a verbal argument as they do to a physical confrontation. Here is danger—fight it or run away from it; there's no time to contemplate facts in this situation. This is why even seemingly benign topics can start heated arguments—our brains aren't trying to evaluate what is best for our holistic growth, and instead are just trying to make sure we *survive*.

And it makes sense, doesn't it? When we began as hunter-gatherers, it was likely important to have group cohesion in opinion or decision-making processes. Disagreements more often did lead to physical confrontation, so the mind had to be ready. As the world and society have progressed, however, the evolution of our brains has not yet kept up, and our tendency to treat our subjective experience as concrete fact actually causes us more harm than benefit.

Let's consider a simple example from my own context. Growing up poor, I used to see certain uses of money as wasteful and impractical. How could someone have the audacity to spend more than seventy dollars a night on a hotel stay? How could they be so impractical as to waste that money on a room they would use for a single night when there were perfectly good Motel 6s all across the country? I thought it foolish to buy sneakers that cost above twenty dollars, as well as higher-costing food or clothing brands. This was using hard-to-come-by capital for frivolous indulgences. If one was so out of touch that they required the more expensive brand of deli meat, I believed them to be detached from the reality of the world around them. I thought they were being wasteful and harming themselves without even knowing it.

This viewpoint came into play when I was a young adult and planned to split a hotel room with a friend of mine for a trip. He was raised in a higher social class background than myself, and we had met in college. During the trip planning, he offered hotel options costing in the hundreds per night. I balked at this and even felt anger at my dear friend. How could he think we should be so wasteful? A bed was a bed, after all. We weren't too good to sleep in whatever situation—we shouldn't waste our money on things that weren't the essentials.

My confusion was met equally with confusion from my pal. He didn't know why I was so upset and was confused as to why we wouldn't invest money in the trip to ensure we enjoyed it to its fullest potential. In his opinion, the hotel room was part of the experience and should be a special treat to be enjoyed. This would be part of our memory-making process.

My social experience had told me that one should never waste money on frivolous additions to a trip. I'd learned that a "nice" room was a selfish indulgence. My friend's social reality entailed investing in the hotel room as a key component of the trip. This money was not to be spent all the time, but a special trip had to be memorable. Both of these social perspectives were influenced by the norms and experiences we had as children growing up in different social classes and family structures. Our initial reactions toward one another were confusion and even a bit of disdain; how could the other person think this way?

The meaning of the cost and its worthiness was being filtered through our own social perspectives. If extra money for a hotel means you can't pay the electric bill, it's outrageous to suggest a higher-priced option. If you have a stable bank account and the cost is seventy dollars more and this is supposed to be a once-in-a-while special trip, why wouldn't you truly enjoy it? We form our initial reactions to these situations by evaluating our own context. For me, that didn't make sense—that would not be a good idea. Therefore, *they* are missing information or are misinterpreting the situation. They are wrong and must understand my insights, which come from my experiences. Now, we don't often actively think this way, but our reactions often follow this chain of logic. Then, all of a sudden, we are putting people into boxes, judging them, and inviting unnecessary conflict into our lives.

In this situation, it was helpful for my friend and me to *listen* as to *why* we each preferred certain hotel options. Once we heard more about our family histories with hotel rooms and the ways in which we were raised, we understood where the other was coming from, found each other reasonable, and approached the planning from a new direction. It wasn't about imposing what we wanted and disregarding the other person, but rather trying to convey what we thought would be best for the entire trip and why.

Let's consider another example that might help illuminate what I mean when I talk about context. The Greek philosopher Plato was famous for his Allegory of the Cave. In this thought experiment, he encouraged the reader to think of a situation where several men had been chained to poles in a cave, their heads stuck facing forward, for their entire lives. They were fed and cared for, but the only thing they could see was the wall right in front of their faces. Their captors would use fire behind them to light up the cavern and cast shadows on the walls, holding up wooden cutouts of animals and making the incorrect noise for each animal. In our example, let's imagine they quacked when they cast a shadow in the shape of a lion.

Now, imagine one day that a prisoner escaped. He left the cave and was startled by what he saw. The sunlight was too bright, the real sights sounds of people and animals very confusing. When he returned to the cave, do you think the other prisoners would believe what he said? That the world was actually lit up by a big bright orb and that there was stuff called grass and a sky and that lions didn't quack, they actually roared?

How do you think the other prisoners would respond?

Plato thought they would call him mad and kill him if they could break free of their chains. They "knew" what the world was like—they'd seen it with their own eyes—and they certainly knew that lions quacked; they'd heard it plenty of times!

Although Plato was talking about universal truths as compared to our limited perceptions, the story works well for describing context. The environments in which we are raised are our caves. Our "captors" are the social groups that portray reality to us—our families, communities, and societies—who cast the shadows by which we understand the world. The "shadows" are the lessons and messages conveyed to us by people, the media, and society. Depending on who we are surrounded by and the messages we are conveying, we perceive different shadows. If someone comes along and tries to tell us that our context is wrong, we sometimes have the same reaction as the prisoners. We believe them to be uninformed, and we desire to be rid of them.

Let's more deeply describe my own "cave." I was raised in Tafton, Pennsylvania, a community near the tourist getaway of Lake Wallenpaupack. The nearest grocery store was eight miles away from my house, the nearest movie theater about twenty, and most of the dining options were in Scranton, about a 45-minute drive down I-84 West. I grew up with raccoons, deer, and bears as my only neighbors. These realities greatly shaped what I view as normal and acceptable.

For example, my wife, who is from suburban New Jersey, is terrified of the woods at night. While I admit nighttime in the woods can be spooky, I constantly remind her of how she is much safer in the woods than in the suburbs. The simple reason for this is that there are no people in the middle of nowhere. Violent crime rates reflect this reality, yet her experience with the woods has been limited throughout her life, and a great deal of her conception of it comes from movies and television shows, where people are attacked and go missing in these areas. These inaccurate depictions and lack of personal experience had her operating in a reality in which she had to be afraid and cautious in rural areas at night.

For those of you who disagree and want to tell us that rural areas are, in fact, unsafe at night, I imagine the first thing you would do is cite an example of a time a violent crime or murder occurred in a rural area. You may even have several cases in mind. Aha! The facts have proven my context wrong and your context right! We will talk about this a little later, but what's happening here is the cherry-picking of certain individual cases or statistics to reinforce a contextual belief system. In short, the contextual beliefs select the facts, rather than the facts determining the contextual belief system. Overall, statistics may support the hypothesis that violent crime rates are lower in rural areas, but those are ignored by people in favor of individual stories that support their original stance or own lived experience.

My wife was a context-breaking individual for me for several reasons, but one is due to the fact that she grew up just outside New York City. Plenty of New Yorkers flooded into the lake region every summer to spend time in their second homes. I thought I knew "city people" because of this experience. They were loud, were bad drivers, caused traffic, complained, and belittled my hometown and all the local people. My complete understanding of New Yorkers was that they were loud, obnoxious, impatient, and impractical. Now, I imagine some of you heartily agree with those descriptors, depending on your experiences, but let me hit you with this last one.

I thought almost all New Yorkers were White. I had absolutely no sense of the diversity of those in the greater New York City Metro area, because a very particular type of tourist group was the one coming to my area and shaping my perspective.

My experience was real, but I was dealing with such a small sliver of New Yorkers (which in this case actually meant those from the city, north Jersey, and Long Island). I also viewed them through a local rural boy's lens. So while I did learn things from this experience, my mind transposed this experience onto an overarching reality. You can imagine how much I scoffed when I heard people refer to it as the greatest city in the world after my time with the tourists.

There are countless more ways I can describe my individual context. I was raised in a two-parent household, so I wasn't shaped by the realities of divorce or single-parent living. My father had challenges with alcohol, and I ended up with strong antidrinking beliefs that pre-vailed until I had my first drink at the age of 23. I grew up in a 95% Caucasian area, limiting my early life exposure to and understanding of people of color. So many of my views of different people and com-munities were shaped by the television and media, which proved to be toxic sources. I went on scholarship to a private university, surrounded by people who looked like me but were from a completely different social class. I've done graduate and professional work in counseling, working with people of all ages from all across the world from all sorts of backgrounds and identities. These experiences in particular had a dramatic influence on my perspective of self, others, and the world overall.

These experiences established the framework through which I view the world. It's important to note, also, that context isn't stagnant. How I viewed myself and others as a child is quite different from how I view those things now. I hope my views in the future are quite different than they are now as well. If I am open to understanding the lived experiences of others, I am open to learning, growing, and developing more wisdom within myself.

There's been a lot of philosophy so far, but what is context, really? Simply put, context is the family, environmental, social, commu-nal, cultural, and societal framework encompassing an individual's lived experience. Social ecological theory states that there are con-centric rings of environmental influence all around us, starting with immediate influences in our life and branching out to societal norms, beliefs, and movements, all of which impact our identity. While con-text is the framework surrounding us, influencing and shaping us, identity is more so how we view ourselves in relation to the contexts around us.

For example, if you live in the United States, you may view yourself as American. Your national context (living in the United States) con-tributes to an aspect of your identity. Being surrounded by American influences (food, social norms, clothing, entertainment options) impacts your identity as well, since you are developing your tastes, style, hob-bies, and relationships all within these contexts. It's straightforward to say that if you were raised in America, you're likely to have some major differences in your beliefs, preferences, and identities than if you were raised in Japan.

Identity is highly influenced by both context and experience. Identity is often at the crux of the reality we live. For example, although a friend of mine was raised in the same home community as me, making her a White American like myself, our lived experience within the United States varies greatly due to the fact that I am straight and she is a lesbian. Her interactions within the contexts of his life are different due to this, as are her experiences in the same settings as myself. The rural conservative town in which I was raised was not widely accepting of LBGTQIA+ individuals during my childhood. My friend, therefore, had a radically different experience with the same social context than I did. My friend also had her view of self negatively influenced by the pervasiveness of negative attitudes toward lesbians.

Let's break this identity piece down even further. I'm going to take a moment and list my top five identifiers. If someone asked me to describe who I am, my identity, in identifiers, this is what I would say, in this order. I encourage you to take a moment before you read my results to write down your own list.

1. Counselor/Professor
2. Writer
3. Husband
4. Rural
5. White Male

Is your list the same as mine? I imagine some of yours are wildly different. There's something fascinating about my list, and it speaks to the huge impact of context. My first three answers are either action-based or relational. Counselor, professor, and writer are professional roles. They are things I choose to do and enjoy doing. They are entirely aspects of a chosen reality. Similarly, husband is the same. It is a major role in my life that I cherish. Only when we get to number four do we see some context, and "rural" as an identifier isn't something I understood until I was an adult and was outside of the rural context. In number five we see something I did not choose, White male, and this gets to the root of all my other responses.

Some of you undoubtedly put gender, sexual orientation, race, or religion higher than number five. As a straight White male in a rural area, I had the privilege to not have the social majority impose labels and identifiers upon me. I was looked at as an individual, in many ways the standard. My context and community norms did not single me out, and thus those aspects of my identity did not ring as salient for me. I had blinders to things like individual culture and race, because the system I lived within did not treat me as "other" in any way. This privilege meant I had significantly fewer social barriers present in my home community than women, individuals of color, or those in the LBGTQIA+ community.

If my community "accepts" me and looks to me as "normal," how much might I relate to this context versus someone who is oppressed by local social systems? It is important to consider what contexts and systems in our lives have favored us and which have disparaged us and others. This is crucial in evaluating who we are, where we feel comfortable, and what we support, and in understanding why others may not have the same experiences, thoughts, and feelings as we do.

As you look at your identity, I encourage you to take a moment to think about how each of your answers influences how you look at the world. Why did you put those answers down? When did you first become aware of those things? How aware of them are you in your daily life? How do those things allow you to connect to other people? How do those things make it a challenge to connect to other types of people?

In short, what's your identity, and where did it come from?

Our identity is a central driving force in our reality. We live and learn from experience, then quickly make judgments, which is helpful to keep us surviving. The most basic form of this is identifying good, bad, safe, and dangerous. This has its advantages in the purely survival sense; however, in society this gets us into several problems. Our brain isn't designed to doubt itself when appraising other people. Just like Anna learned to treat all challenges as severe threats, someone may see a media portrayal of a group of people (let's say a Fox News segment on liberals), and their brain may look at that and say, "Those are dangerous people."

Our mind values and reinforces our identity and experiences. It dismisses and diminishes the experiences of others. When I talk about this in context, I don't only mean the big issues (social class, race, religion, sexuality, and so on), but I mean the simple everyday experience. Have you ever experienced a similar situation to the following?

"I love Jay's Restaurant; they have the best food in town!"

"Ugh, what are you talking about? That place sucks! I went and my chicken was severely undercooked."

Or how about ...

"I love the latest Tom Cruise movie! It was filled with action every moment."

"Ugh, are you kidding me? Poor writing and more plot holes than I could count."

In the first example, someone has had positive experiences with Jay's Restaurant. Their experience has led them to link being a fan of Jay's with a small part of their identity. Their praise represents their opinion and dining habits. This is met with a conflicting reality of someone who had a negative experience at Jay's.

One could argue whether or not Jay's is good based on multiple reviews, but the reality is, each of these two people had different experiences. For the person who had a negative experience, this is their entire reality of Jay's Restaurant. Therefore, to them, Jay's is bad. Now, we could say that perhaps this person should give Jay's a second shot. But sometimes this person would be met with a negative comment, suggesting they hadn't given it a full shot, had gotten the wrong menu item, had been too picky, or simply had chosen the wrong night. This type of response moves the focus away from their experience and toward criticism of their emotional processing and beliefs around this experience. In short, it often makes someone feel criticized or feel badly for simply feeling what they did about something. As we mentioned earlier, this isn't helpful, since our brains start acting like they are in a physical confrontation. And in a way, our brains are protecting us. We all wish to be *represented* through our preferences and recommendations—none of us want to exist in a reality where we have poor judgment and tastes. Fighting off the conflicting opinion of another or dismissing their ideas through personal attacks therefore makes complete sense as a defensive mechanism.

In the second example, one person enjoys the movie because of the action, excitement, stunts, and pacing. It's likely they have enjoyed their experience with this style of entertainment throughout their life. The second person, although experiencing the same movie, has a completely different lens on the experience, valuing writing structure over action. You'll see this type of conflicting reality pop up online, where people debate the merits of movies and video games. People with diverging opinions are often dismissed with high levels of disparaging comments and insults. This is because the individuals arguing are *not* arguing about the merits of a movie. Instead, they are defending their own lived experience and preferences, a facet of their very identity. This conflict and defense are what make something so seemingly innocuous, such as a movie preference, something that can, and time after time does, translate into online death threats.

A simple example is the *Star Wars* fan base. There is a small but vocal contingency of *Star Wars* fans who viciously demean the inclusion of a more diverse cast, including the female lead of the latest trilogy portrayed by Daisy Ridley. In their mind, *Star Wars* represents something to them. What they've created *Star Wars* to mean and how they integrate their fandom into their identity is very important to them—thus they lash out at anything that threatens their reality and identity as they've constructed it. They would rather the creative property be only what they've made meaning of it as and thus decry society for altering something they view as sacred.

We'll touch on this later, but a key idea to remember is this: *The less one has critically examined and explored their own identity and insecurities, the more they are likely to lash out at others who have different opinions or interpretations.* In short, if we don't love what's left after we strip away some of what we've chosen to identify ourselves, we're going to fight like hell to preserve our image of how things were.

There are two more simple examples that demonstrate the intertwined relationship between identity and context. I have a friend who is a huge fan of the band The Rolling Stones. The same is true of his three siblings. They believe that this band is the best there is and can cite plenty of examples why. Curiously, their parents were also huge Rolling Stones fans. What are the odds, when there are so many thousands upon thousands of bands in existence, that the entire family all independently decides this *single* band is the greatest?

Likewise, somehow this entire family all held the *same* religion. Again—what are the odds? Out of the thousands upon thousands of religions, each of these people came together and decided that Catholicism is the one true path? What luck and fortune they all ended up together as a family unit.

You'll sense my sarcasm throughout the above example. These are realities we see every day, but oddly, we never question them. My friend is both Catholic and a fan of The Rolling Stones because of the family he was born into—because of the context in which he was raised. It influenced his understanding of what was proper, correct, and enjoyable. If he'd been born into a family who loved Green Day, for example, odds are he might be more favorable to their music than The Rolling Stones. If he'd been born in Pakistan, a majority Islamic nation, odds are much more likely he'd be a Muslim. It's interesting to me that we live every day considering that we ourselves are largely situationally derived and conversely treat others who are different as being fundamentally flawed.

Let's consider religion a little more. I recall one time, as a child, I had a conversation with a schoolmate about the nature of God. I was perhaps 10 or 11 when this conversation occurred. He was raised in a highly religious household, whereas I was not. I asked him what he thought about God—could God be this, that, or the other thing? I particularly remember suggesting (cleverly, I thought) that perhaps the earth was a cell within the great body of God and that we were all microorganisms.

This classmate chuckled and shook his head with disdain. He thought it was funny how foolish and uninformed I was. He went on to explain the Holy Trinity to me, despite the fact I was well aware of what this was. When I acknowledged that yes, that could be true, but what if it wasn't, he looked at me, puzzled. He politely informed me that that was impossible, that he was correct, and that I needed to accept the truth. I again stated something like, "Yes, you could be right and I could be wrong, but what do you think about these other possibilities?" Again, he shook his head, sighed, and said something about how that would be a waste of time and brain energy. The truth was already known, and I shouldn't waste time thinking about anything else.

Religion has always fascinated me for this reason. It is a context largely given to children through their families. It provides connection to family, community, and a definition of purpose. It therefore makes sense to me why it could be hard for someone to question religion, because it's not the facts they are questioning but major foundational tenets of their *entire* identity! My classmate (and others of varying religious backgrounds I have spoken to over the years) could not even entertain the idea that their faith had missed some points or could be wrong in some ways. Religion can be so beautiful for people, and my intention was never to convince people that they were wrong. However, it was always stark to me how some could not even *consider* questions around these belief systems, illustrating their role in forming the person's individual "cave" and context. Those who tended to have the biggest commitment to and understanding of their religion, in my opinion, where those people I met over the years who did critically analyze their faith. They were the ones who were able to digest the question "What if this is wrong, or what if there is no God?" They did not feel threatened or destroyed by these questions but thoughtful and empowered through the spiritual journey it took them on in affirming their beliefs.

The major takeaway here is this: So much of who we are is not a product of individual achievement or intellectual realization but is instead the result of the random conditions of our upbringing, instilling values and beliefs in us without our conscious awareness. Our minds aren't quite built to critically examine ourselves in this way, however, instead assuming that our experiences are real, proper experiences founded in truth and that everyone else is unaware of these things. Tribalistic identities were once incredibly helpful as survival mechanisms, and since society has changed pace at a much faster rate than religion, it makes complete sense that these reactions are still hardwired into us. This doesn't mean, however, we can't begin becoming more self-aware and challenging them to live more peacefully each day.

There are counterpoints to the above, most pointedly that some people go the complete opposite way of their parents, and some people completely doubt themselves and what they think about the world. This, too, is a product of identity; if at a young age we identify as being close with or similar to our parents, we're more likely to take on these beliefs. If we have a difficult family life or a major event that causes us to split from our parents, we may be more likely to reject that contextual reality and believe that it is wrong.

For example, individuals in my extended family had challenges with alcohol when I was a child. My context then shaped a reality for me. My context became this: Alcohol is bad, and people only drink it to avoid themselves and their problems. My truth became this: People only drink to get drunk, no good comes from alcohol, and it's a betrayal to the self to consume it. While I did not identify with some of the contextual framework surrounding me, it undoubtedly majorly influenced my identity, outlook, and life steps.

Likewise, doubting one's own ability, opinions, and worth is in itself a belief. I've met plenty of people who would claim they aren't intelligent and that they have lousy opinions, yet when I counter them with my authentic conception of them as intelligent, thoughtful, and worthwhile, they argue against this. While they said they were wrong, they fought against me to *prove* they were wrong. They believed that I was unaware of deeper truths about them that they had gathered from their lived context and experience—a context and experience that had made them associate their identity with being lesser. Our minds try to be "correct" more than they try to be truly happy, and this is something we will touch on later.

For now, let's dive into the counseling perspective from which I'm viewing many of these things. In introducing the counseling perspective and principles, I'm hopeful you can see how counselors encourage positive growth and can utilize some of these principles in your day-to-day life.

Counseling is performed by an individual trained most often in one of three disciplines: psychology, social work, or counseling. Psychology takes a *diagnostic* approach to mental health—what is wrong, and what is the diagnosis? Social work takes a *systemic approach*—what systems are influencing the challenges, and what can be changed? Counseling takes a *humanistic approach*—how can I help someone find their own answers and solutions?

Many mainstream counseling approaches are influenced by Carl Rogers's person-centered therapeutic approach, particularly using his concept of unconditional positive regard. This approach focuses on the relationship in the counseling setting, putting heavy emphasis on the partnership between counselor and client. The counselor's major role is to provide a space where the client feels safe, valued, and understood. Rather than being an "expert," the counselor is more of a facilitator of change, supporting the client in finding their own answers.

Research shows that positive rapport between counselor and client itself leads to positive outcomes and growth. Regardless of therapeutic style or intervention, a positive relationship positively correlates with client wellness and growth. If we listen to and care about people, they will be willing to challenge themselves and their perspectives and work through issues on their own. Think of it as giving someone a supportive foundation to stand on as they work through difficult issues in their life.

This ties into the concept of unconditional positive regard within person-centered therapy. Unconditional positive regard is exactly what it sounds like: the counselor expresses positive sentiments about the client regardless of who the client is or their behavior. Now, positive does not mean always encouraging. For example, a counselor should challenge some clients' behaviors or express concern. Unconditional positive regard more so means the counselor makes it clear they are not judging the client in a negative fashion. They care about and support the client and are there to help them change. Even if the client has a regression, makes a mistake, or reveals something shameful about themselves, the counselor will still be there as a supportive partner in the therapeutic process. Think of this as the counselor saying, "I like you, and I'm here for you no matter what."

Unconditional positive regard establishes a relationship where people feel understood. They feel heard and supported and thus are more willing to dive deeper into what they are going through. They are more willing to be challenged because they realize they are not being judged and will not lose the relationship. We establish rapport and regard as a foundation to fall back on when it's time to point out the client's incongruence between wants and behaviors. We challenge them when we point out that perhaps they could have made other choices, or perhaps they have a role in a toxic relationship. The client sees that the counselor is *not trying to judge or put the client down but is instead looking out for them and trying to help them find answers.*

Think of how it would feel if you could speak to someone and say whatever you truly think and feel without having to dress it up or leave any details out. Your thoughts, feelings, passions, shortcomings, failures, doubts—anything and everything you think and feel. You can just say it and be accepted. Fully accepted—no caveats. Think of how rare this is for us. We are so relationally driven. We feel we must appear or act a certain way to get along in society, whether at work or with friends and family. For those we are close to, we don't want to complicate the relationship with messy details and feelings. We're so worried about how we appear that we repress who we truly are. If only we could live with more unconditional positive regard for ourselves and others in daily life, where we could listen, care, learn, and grow together.

This is a crucial concept in what we will cover in this book. Think about everyday life situations in which people challenge one another, whether it is over opinions, preferences, actions, or life roles. What happens in these situations? People feel *attacked* and *judged*. They look at the other person as someone who is *putting them down*, or at the very least raining on their parade.

Take a moment to reflect on online arguments on Facebook and Twitter. People challenge one another with examples and facts and are stunned to see the "irrational other" reject their claims and come back with insults. There is no common understanding. There is no positive regard. There are simply people attacking and defending. The ideas and facts are not considered or taken in, because why would they be?

The other person simply seems to be trying to win a victory over them. They're just trying to be right and make them look wrong. Why in the world would someone listen with an open mind and heart to someone who treats them in this way?

An example I have seen with students is a client who has a difficult relationship with an overbearing and emotionally abusive mother. There are times when a counselor will be able to identify a core issue with a client early in the relationship. In this example, within the very first session, the counselor sees that the client is participating in a relationship where she is giving her mother too much power and influence in her life, and this is majorly adding to her stress and depression. So what should the counselor do? Tell this observation to the client? Tell her that her relationship with her mother isn't healthy and that this is what they need to work on? List for her what the counselor has observed and how it is detrimental to wellness? Give examples of what these toxic, codependent relationships look like and cite figures about how they facilitate depression?

In this example, these things may be spot-on, true observations. They may be what is occurring in reality; however, they are some of the *last* things I suggest the counselor say. This approach is likely to be highly ineffective and may even result in the client abandoning therapy.

How in the world can we expect someone to accept this from us after knowing us for less than an hour? How could they trust these insights at all? Won't her initial reaction be something akin to *How can this person judge my relationship with my mother? How can they say something is wrong with me? I didn't come here to talk about my mom, and they are trying to make it about her!*

If the client isn't directly talking about mom, she probably either isn't aware of the dynamic or isn't ready to deal with it. If she's not aware, she's going to get defensive and resist the direction of the counselor— our minds naturally try to stay in the "safe," understood reality in which we are living. Think of it as a blanket we thought was keeping us safe but instead has been slowly suffocating us the whole time. The known is comfortable and repeatedly reinforced by our minds, even if it is not helpful.

The truth and facts are not effective instruments of growth or change in this example. The counselor asserting their insights in this situation is an action that is not taken in the best interests of the client. It is instead the counselor expressing something they know for their own benefit. It feels good to notice and point out things—it feels good to be right. But if the client isn't ready for this, our efforts will likely result in her digging deeper into their thought patterns, pushing her further away from the growth and change she needs.

What should the counselor do? Well, certainly we're going to get to the relationship with her mother, just *not right now*. Instead, let's work on *understanding* what the client thinks is important. Let's *understand* and *validate* her family situation and her relationship with her mother. Let's express some *empathy* over her difficulties and ask what *she sees* as major things to work on. Let's *give her a voice* so she feels *heard* and *represented*. In short, we're giving her the space to *express her reality and let it be accepted before we attempt to alter it together*.

Once this happens and we dive more into Mom in later sessions, our questions or observations are likely to bring forward new realizations. This is because the client trusts us, the defensive walls are lowered, and she's willing to consider a new interpretation of the relationship. This isn't just a hypothetical example; I've done and seen similar work with many clients.

So how does this apply to non-counselors? I stress what counselors do because so often in our lives we try to *impose* our reality on others. We argue preferences, beliefs, and approaches to everyday life situations and then are frustrated and upset when we are unable to get through to someone. We feel divided as a nation, isolated in our own bubbles, and disconnected from family and friends. Is it any surprise anxiety and depression rates continue to rise?

If we are to navigate through an increasingly divided world, we need to begin considering what methods and approaches are effective for communication and joint understanding, and what methods simply drive people further away from us. In order for us to avoid the pain that comes with these conflicts, we need to consider our own motives in trying to convince others, reflect on our own feelings about ourselves and the situation, and completely change our approach. There are ways to effectively be ourselves and communicate with others, but these things often require an understanding of self and others that most of us are unwilling to acquire.

I'll give you an example that relates back to the counseling role. Having unconditional positive regard seems straightforward enough, but what if the client is someone you personally dislike? What if they are someone who does heinous things? I've worked with students who were vicious bullies and others who exhibited behaviors of sexual predators, attempting to groom younger students. Certainly, my personal feelings toward these students are not positive. Their actions conflict with my values, yet I approached them with unconditional positive regard.

The bullies turned out to be students who came from dysfunctional households, many suffering emotional and physical abuse at home, who were struggling for moments of control in lives spiraling out of it. It was certainly not an excuse for their behavior, but rather the reason, and once this came to light, all of a sudden they were willing to truly hear the impact of what they were doing. They were willing to face themselves, no longer hiding behind defensive walls, and deal with the shame that came with their actions. Once who they were was understood and put out in the open, they were willing to see and understand who others were and what they were going through. And slowly but surely, things changed at the school.

Part of me may have been tempted to put them down. Why should the perpetrator in this situation receive any kindness? These are our natural reactions, but my job was not to exact vengeance but instead encourage positive change—for the bullies and everyone in the school. These methods required me to be patient and to listen in ways I was not always naturally inclined to. We must ask ourselves—do we want to punish the bullies, or do we want them to change? Do we want vengeance, or do we want actual positive improvement in the school?

The students who exhibited predatory behavior were another challenge. How could I treat them in a kind manner? How could I play card games with them during our chats? Draw pictures? Laugh and goof around? Weren't they the monsters of society?

Monsters and the concept of "the other" are central in how we deal with others. The things sexual predators do are heinous and reviling, so much so that we desperately avoid the reality that *given the proper conditions, any one of us could be exactly like them.*

This is a controversial statement and one we consistently try to avoid by simply calling them "monsters." This dismisses our shared humanity, declares us as something separate from them, and is very comfortable. We do this with offenders but also with those different from us.

"This political group is hopeless—they don't listen to facts and act like a cult!" This statement inherently dismisses people as "other." They cannot be reached and are something different. They are irrational or damaged beyond repair. These statements aren't about making progress and fixing the problem but rather are self-serving statements fulfilling the purpose of reinforcing our own comfortable reality—I am good and they are bad. This type of thinking keeps us ingrained in our trenches, robbing us of the ability to connect with others and grow personally.

For example, I once worked with a client who had experienced extensive, brutal sexual abuse throughout his childhood from his caregivers. What did he understand about relationships and sexuality? What thoughts and impulses were ingrained in him due to these experiences? Certainly, if I had lived through what he had, wouldn't I also have severe emotional maladjustment? Isn't it possible that I, too, would develop sexual impulses linked to control and power?

If I was to help him work through these feelings and not act on them, I had to provide him a safe, supportive atmosphere where he could express what he'd gone through, as well as what he was dealing with. It is easy to judge and shame others for our own purposes, but if I was going to help him, and thereby *anyone at risk from being around him*, I had to focus on what was effective.

I showed understanding to him. I validated that what he had lived through was real—what he'd gone through had formed these reactions in him. We were operating within his reality (he was not "the other"), and he became willing to work through his feelings. He became willing to adjust and monitor his behavior. I cannot for certain speak to his full sincerity, nor can I guarantee he will remain a nonpredator, but what I can say is that this approach was more effective than shaming or judging, which would have simply encouraged him to develop his fantasies secretly, away from the eyes of anyone who could help.

We have to ask ourselves this: When we are expressing our opinion, are we in good faith trying to guide or help someone, or are we imposing our values for our own sake? Are we trying to be positive and make a difference in the world, or are we trying to feel a moment of superiority? If we are trying to feel superiority, what don't we like about ourselves, our lives, or how we relate to the world, and how can we heal? If we are not considering the position we are coming from, what our context and experiences are, can we truly have a grasp on the effectiveness of our communication? Is this pattern of communication helpful and healthy to our own lives? Is what we're doing really the "right" thing just because we're expressing the "right" opinion, or is there more nuance to consider?

Let's jump into that now, as we look at just how and why we impose our context upon others.

chapter three

How We Impose Our Context on Others

Harkening back to earlier examples, isn't it fascinating that most people born and raised in Philadelphia are fans of Philadelphia sports teams? How did they objectively decide that these teams were "the best" or most deserving of their fandom? Haven't they been made aware of the unsavory behavior of other Philly sports fans, such as booing Santa Claus and throwing batteries?

Sports team fandom is an interesting phenomenon. People like to argue over which team is best, which team will win, which players are the best (both currently and throughout history), and as you've noticed, people take these interactions quite seriously. There are heated arguments, violence, and even murders committed due to escalations around these topics. But doesn't that seem strange?

It isn't as if the people arguing this are *actually* part of the team. They aren't the players. They aren't involved in the performance of the team or any of its functions. They don't truly have *any* stake in the outcome of the game, barring any gambling commitments. So why, then, do people care about these things so much?

Sports fandom is not about the actual objective reality of the sports teams. Individuals argue which team is the best, for example, "the Patriots and Steelers have won six Super Bowls!" But this can be argued against using the fact that the Packers have 13 total NFL championships. But then we are likely to have Dolphins, Bears, and 49ers fans claim that the 1972, 1985, and 1989 teams, respectively, are the best single team to ever take the field—making their franchises the best. So here we have objective facts being presented, but the argument isn't truly about the objective reality. We have fans from different contexts using different facts in different ways to justify their inherent standing. The facts are merely tools used to reinforce an identity within a context; each of the fans in these examples wants their team to be considered the best, or at least to downplay the greatness of another franchise.

Why are these fans trying to impose their reality upon others? Why do they dismiss fans of other teams, labeling them as classless or ignorant, sure signs they are viewing them as "other"? The answer is that sports fandom is rarely about anything related to the game itself. It is related to context and identity.

These people are fans of teams from their home regions, or perhaps they are fans due to a family affiliation or a choice they made as a child. They seek identity in the fact that they affiliate themselves with a sports team. Therefore, they are represented by their fandom and by the performance of the team. The team doing well represents them well, giving them power and success. Being "right" in their opinion about the best team or players puts them above "the other," who is looking at the "facts" in the wrong manner. This is an inherent position that most of our minds take: *What I realize and believe is right and what others realize and believe is wrong.*

Sports teams are a way in which we *create* our identity from within the contexts we were raised. We certainly have a degree of choice in supporting which team and to what degree, but still these concepts become integrated into our identities. "I'm an Eagles fan" is something I say when talking about the NFL to other people. This statement, in particular the "I am" portion, indicates that I relate to a group, considering myself to be part of it and it to be part of me.

Our minds are designed to *defend* our identity and perspectives. In the state of nature into which we were born, believing in one's opinions and actions was often necessary to survive. Our mind therefore will viciously protect aspects of our identity. This is why people argue so much over sports—they are not fighting about the teams but defending aspects of their identity. They are standing up for their group and reality and imposing its truths upon "the other."

The less secure someone is in their life and identity, the more likely they are to become heated about things like sports team preferences. They may not have many other aspects of their identity that they enjoy, value, or are confident in; thus they put much emotional stock into this aspect of their identity. Any challenge to this is therefore a major challenge to their entire created image, and the idea of that being *wrong* or *bad* is a major existential problem, which most people do not want to face. After all, who wants to be *wrong* or *stupid* in who they are and what they believe in?

Existentialism is a European philosophical tradition expounded on by thinkers such as Kierkegaard, Nietzsche, Sartre, de Beauvoir, and Camus, which has influenced some counseling approaches, most notably existential therapy, detailed in depth by Irvin Yalom. Major tenants of existentialism include isolation and meaninglessness. Isolation speaks to the belief that we truly are isolated and alone. Namely, it means I can only be myself—I cannot literally become one with another person, despite my attempts to role-play this through social interaction.

Meaninglessness, or nothingness, speaks to some of the tenets of social constructivism we discussed earlier, namely that there is nothing innate about the world in which we live. These tenets claims that we come into the world without a true purpose or meaning—meaning and purpose are things we are responsible to create through our own freedom. We constantly wish to avoid the overarching nothingness—the anxiety that comes with the fact that we aren't innately defined and may not have a life purpose or afterlife destination.

Now, depending on your worldview, you may wholly reject that notion, and that is fine. However, its tenets ring true in much of what we see in the world. In the sports fan example, some individuals may construct and create meaning in their fandom. It may play a major role in their identity, relationships, and meaningful life traditions. This is something they are *creating* and a meaning they are *instilling* in their lives. Thus, if this aspect of their identity is challenged ("How could you be a Cowboys fan?" or "How could you waste so much money on tailgates and season tickets?"), they are likely to become defensive. They are likely to cite the validity of their life and the meaning that comes from their fandom.

If we threaten to take away key concepts of people's constructed identities (fandoms, relationships, political beliefs, spiritual beliefs, professional roles, etc.), they are likely to become very defensive to avoid *losing their identity*. This ties into the existential principle of avoiding nothingness. If I attacked the validity of your life relationships, and everything you love and believe, and you ended up siding with my attacks, where would that leave you? Who would you be? Our minds desperately do not wish to go there; thus, anything that is interpreted as an attack on our context and reality is usually met with strong defensive measures. Thus, people use the objective (in the sports case, various facts) to *justify their contextual stance.* Facts do not speak to me and prove to me that the Cowboys are the best team, but rather I seek facts in the world that justify and reinforce my *initial standing based on my context.*

This links to the concept of confirmation bias, or the psychological principle that shows that people pay much greater attention to information that confirms their preexisting beliefs while minimizing or dismissing factual evidence that counters their stances. For example, if an individual has the racist viewpoint that "all minorities are dangerous," they are likely to be able to cite and recall news stories wherein crimes were perpetrated by minorities, using this as clear evidence proving their original viewpoint. They are likely to either not remember or to dismiss news stories that represent minorities with positive characteristics or actions. These do not play into their constructed narrative and therefore are often not added to their memory banks. While this example is easy to understand, we must note that essentially all of us do this, and it is a human faculty. This is why major media corporations have slants—it is very marketable to provide stories that people will consume as "proof" and "validation" of who they are and what they believe.

Confirmation bias directly plays a role in how we interpret information in the world around us. Studies have shown that people consistently rank studies that have conclusions in line with their own opinion as being of superior quality to those that have opposing conclusions. Further, people have a tendency to rank candidates from opposing political parties as having inconsistent statements, even when their own candidate has just as many or even more inconsistent statements. We are likely to give the benefit of the doubt to facts and people we believe represent us, while we do not do the same for groups we consider "other." This allows us to put up walls and dig into our own beliefs, assured we are "right" while "the other" is wrong, causing many problems in our society. You'll notice this is highly prevalent in political discussions—how often do we see someone call out another for being biased, while seeming to completely avoid or even be unaware of the massive amount of bias they are exhibiting in the interaction?

This ties back to the existential principles. We are subtly aware of the social construct and the order of things. We understand that other people have different opinions, and some of our preferences truly can't be proven or accepted as the overall right way. We see that there is power in someone believing or doubting us. A quick example: A child who is bullied and told they are bad by other students may internalize the socially constructed opinion that they are bad. We implicitly understand that so much of our truth is constructed or situational; thus, we desperately want to avoid the power of others to make us into something.

I saw a YouTube video that illustrated this effectively. In it, two children are arguing over whether it is "raining" or "drizzling" outside. One child is defensive because his parent told him that it was only drizzling, so he confronts the other child with this fact. Both argue heatedly about whether it is raining or drizzling—both trying to impose their interpreted constructed realities. We smile, laugh, and shake our heads at children when they do this, yet we are doing it all the time as adults.

We are dismayed when others disagree with us or refute us because we understand that their power of social interpretation has an impact on who we are. How they view us makes us something lesser in their eyes, and we want to avoid that. Have you ever seen this on social media? When someone posts their political opinion and is met with refutations? People rejecting their perspective and calling them this, that, or the other thing? We see people on these posts backed into corners, their arguments and "facts" not having the intended impact. We may see others truly get the one-up on them in the "fact" department, and then what happens?

They delete the post. The original poster does not want to be made into something. They don't want to be "misunderstood" or "not accepted." They wanted their assertion of identity to stick and be validated, and instead others were using their freedom to view the poster as something they did not want to be. It's either deletion or blocking—a way to completely remove "the other" and not have to deal with the difficult emotions of conflicting realities.

We fight for our opinions online. We try and assert who we are. We're quick to provide counterexamples from our lived experience that show that the reality they are trying to convey isn't the truth. In the short run, these strategies can be effective. We feel a rush of dopamine for "proving" the other wrong. We can avoid reflecting on who we really are deep down where these opinions came from, how we can grow, and what we really need. There is comfort and simplicity in our brain's natural reactions, but in a complex society with an ever-growing amount of exposure to communication, these tendencies lead to more conflict, stress, anxiety, and depression.

Numerous studies indicate that social media use and exposure correlate with increased levels of anxiety and depression. We see high levels of confirmation bias and defensiveness when people immediately criticize these conclusions. People who use social media often do not want to feel as if it is "bad" or "harmful," since it is part of their identity and how they view themselves. For those of us who have seen the articles laying out the research on this topic, I'm sure we've seen comments expressing, "Well, it's more likely that people who are *already* sad and anxious are retreating to social media"—which undoubtedly happens, but this fails to account for the fact that researchers have certainly controlled for that reality in their study and have still found that the findings hold.

And doesn't it make sense that social media usage would cause more anxiety and depression? Think about it—what kind of stories get the most traffic online? News stories about tragedies and scandals circulate. All of a sudden we have access to almost every major tragic event the world has to offer. Despite the fact that, statistically, murder and crime are down and the standard of living has steadily increased across the entire world, and there are plenty of measures and studies to prove this, people feel that the world is becoming a worse and more dangerous place to live.

What effect will that have?

We receive exposure to every bit of bad news in the world, where in the past this never happened. We enter online communities where there is constant, vicious bickering and bullying. We try to represent our lives in an "ideal" way to get shares and likes, to so often not get the attention we desire, or to see others become more successful. Operating in this reality, where success equals fleeting moments of attention, will undoubtedly affect one's emotional state. The temporary boost that comes with the online interaction isn't likely to transition into the other moments of our lives. The rest of our lives may in fact feel empty—and we may crave the slight dopamine hit that comes with seeing we have another like on our post.

And even still, I can hear the arguments against what I am saying. What is interesting is this: None of what I am saying takes away the reality for many that social media is a positive experience. For those of marginalized backgrounds, it is a portal to find empowerment and connections—a true community. For others, it's a perfect way to maintain loving friendships and family relationships. It can bring joy, give a needed distraction, and empower necessary political movements. All these things can be lived realities while an overarching reality also exists in which, for many people, social media is a detriment. We'd like to make our lived experience, whatever it is, more representative of the overarching reality.

This is why I talk about existentialism. A key concept of Sartre's philosophy is the gaze of the other. This is what we mentioned earlier, namely that we become uncomfortable when stared at by other people. We realize that they are thinking about us, drawing opinions and judgments about who we are or our behavior. They are *making* us into something we do not want to be. We are forced to become aware that we exist as an *object* in their world, rather than us existing entirely independent of others. We realize we are objects, and thus Sartre claims we often objectify ourselves—identifying ourselves with roles, images, and created norms.

Think of online quizzes that identify you with a character or group— the example of the Harry Potter house-sorting quizzes comes to mind. In these quizzes, you answer questions related to personality traits and preferences linked to the Harry Potter universe, and the quiz sorts you into one of the four houses of Hogwarts. People love to share these results—either championing their group as the best or decrying how their results are inaccurate as to who they are. There are all sorts of these quizzes, and they receive a great deal of traffic; we're all eager to find something to *represent* us.

Speaking of representation, let's talk about marketing. Ads represent individuals who use products in a certain way. Archetypes of manly men driving certain types of pickup trucks or cool celebrities preferring certain products permeate our society. We wear shirts designed from elements of our favorite television shows, movies, and food products. We choose clothing that overall we feel *represents* us—which is clearly demonstrated in the models chosen to wear clothing in different stores. Businesses are aware that we *craft a social identity through choices in leisure, brands, and clothing;* thus, they adapt their marketing style to fit just that.

This type of person uses this product. This type of success is linked to this clothing. *Build and represent your identity through our product— not theirs.* Brand loyalty is often less about defending the quality or uniqueness of the brand and more so adhering to the belief that we make the right choices and represent how a life should be lived.

These are exact examples of social construction. We piece together how we represent ourselves with items from the world around us. Clothes, styles, cars, consumer choices, political opinions, bumper stickers—all of these things are a way for us to convey a message to the world. *This is who I am, this is what I believe, and this is how I'm right.*

Language is the vehicle by which we navigate social construction. This is why people are affected by insults and name-calling; language *makes us something* in the reality of another. Language is what conveys *meaning* and can be used to *put us into boxes.* For example, let's think of a current social challenge: people refusing to call transgender or non-gender-conforming individuals by their preferred pronouns.

Why does this matter? Well, in choosing to be transphobic and using the improper pronouns, a person is *denying the reality of a person who identifies as transgender.* They are negating the person's identity and setting the stage for others to do the same. Language is a tool transgender people have to express their reality and lived experience. Pronouns allow expression of individuality and control over one's own identity and image. Taking this away from a person is harmful, telling them that *who they are is wrong and an objectively wrong expression.* And why would someone claim that a transgender individual is wrong? Well, that person's existence challenges their own contextual bias—they believed their experience with and definitions of gender were absolute, they want their context to be the overarching reality, and thus they malign anyone who is an exception to that framework.

We can see why, with these stakes, there are so many movements around sensitivity and awareness of proper pronouns. Language is the building block of social construction and identity. Social concepts come from the use and understanding of shared language. This is why using improper pronouns is not just harmful in the individual case—it sets a precedent for others in society to disregard people who identify as transgender. Improper usage in television and media *creates* a social reality others can conform to, accepting a harmful act and interpretation.

Language is a central concept in narrative therapy, building on social constructivist principles. In narrative therapy, a client is encouraged to search for themes in their life story. They are encouraged to rework interpretations of difficult times and events, "editing" chapters and plotting out how the story will progress from this point forward. It is an empowering therapeutic style that encourages the client to realize they have the power to interpret, tell, and write their own narrative in life. This therapy is particularly relevant, in my opinion, because of how often we are telling stories and creating an image of who we are.

We are the main character in our own story, but we don't like to think about how we are a secondary, background, or even unmentioned character in the lives of countless others. Think of how often we are eager to share details about ourselves, things we know or have experienced. We're just waiting for our next line, because we're the protagonist in our own minds!

We are creating our "main character" through many actions in our lives. We try to take control of how that character is looked on and represented. My favorite example of this is Twitter profiles. Think of the taglines you see under people's names on the website. Artist. Innovator. Entrepreneur. Mother. Daughter. Leader, Republican, Democrat, etc., etc., etc.

These are combinations of objectifying concepts—people choosing to identify themselves with relational roles or actions. This comes from a desire for others to understand a constructed identity. We want to avoid being completely objectified and made into something by others; thus, we take on roles and identities to represent ourselves. Many of these things aren't innate—we aren't born as entrepreneurs, nor are we imbued with the essential essence of one. Our life roles can quickly change, yet we want to be *known* and *represented*.

Think of it: Social media influencers make entire careers out of asserting they are this, that, or the other thing and convincing other people it's true. Their repeated attempts at social representation eventually transition into a reality. The fake-it-till-you-make-it principle is in full effect!

This is just an example of how we impose our context. We use our identities to draw an initial line in others' interpretations about us. This is also why people, in general, enjoy posting profile pictures in which they look the most attractive rather than those that may be more representative of how they commonly look. We want others to objectify us in a *positive* way, with their impression making us an *attractive person*.

Online communities also represent how created communities come together in shared understandings of created realities. Think of this in terms of the "bubbles" that exist online. Depending on your online connections, for example, you're likely to be exposed to wildly different sources of media. If we scrolled down the Twitter feed of someone who is, say, a far-right Republican, I imagine we would see many posts discussing the sins of the Left. We would get specific news stories, angles, and spins. We'd get certain memes, humor, and entertainers. There would be other people, often with the exact same views, sharing their agreements and takes on these things. They would support one another and confirm this shared reality.

If we did the same with someone on the far Left, we'd likely have completely different news stories, coverage, memes, issues discussed, and overall conclusions. The two bubbles would each have completely different stories and narratives playing out, each appalled that the other side hasn't heard about this, that, or the other thing, and each baffled that the other side cares about this or that insignificant story. There are figures on each of these two sides that have hundreds of thousands or even millions of active followers who people in the other bubble have never heard of. Think about that—we have highly influential figures and media stories reaching millions, which millions of others have absolutely no sense of.

Online interaction allows us to gravitate toward realities that match our preferences and confirm our biases. This is easy and comfortable, since here we find facts, validation, and agreement for who we are, how we think, and how we act. This reinforces our brain's natural tendency to assert our identity, dismiss the other, and be "right." We have unlimited access to "facts" and people willing to tell us we are "right."

This plays out in significant ways in our everyday lives. People who never interact with the "other" can fully define who they are, why they are wrong, and what they need to do differently. Numerous research studies have shown that Democrats and Republicans, for example, have a difficult time correctly identifying the sociocultural characteristics of the opposing party. Both groups tend to overestimate the percentage of the party who are different than themselves and attribute the other party members with beliefs that are not commonly held. When living in media bubbles only portraying the most extreme examples of the "other" individuals tend to make generalizations about those different than themselves which solidify as deeply held beliefs. These beliefs lead to conflict and insults which the other side sometimes does not even understand.

Thus, here we are, living in a divisive society, each of us attempting to impose who we are but also impose our reality on "the other," dismissing them as biased, misled, ignorant, the enemy—something beyond reason or reach. Something we fail to realize when operating in this sense is the contingency of context—namely, that we very easily could be the *exact same thing as the person we despise.*

The common phrase "One man's terrorist is another man's freedom fighter" comes to mind to particularly illustrate this point. The phrase speaks to the idea that, depending on the nation or group you are in, actions may be looked at as evil and terroristic or necessary and heroic. Let's examine our wars in the Middle East, for example. To many Americans, guerrilla fighters using RPGs and land mines to sneak-attack troops is heinous and cowardly. In their minds, here is the evil "other" assaulting representations of freedom and liberty in defense of their vile systems. I doubt, however, that those fighters see themselves as evil, and in fact see the Americans as the evil "other." They likely view a major world power that has intervened in the affairs of other nations, including keeping a constant military presence, resulting in untold innocent civilian casualties, as the representation of pure evil, akin to the Empire within the Star Wars universe. In their minds, they are likely the freedom fighters, the plucky rebels sacrificing their lives for a greater good in a struggle against the ultimate evil.

You undoubtedly have reactions to that scenario, or objections based on how I represented it, facts that come to your mind to disprove or at least correct some of what I said—and this is my point. Your context determines which interpretation you see as valid, what facts come to mind, and what facets of your experience you can use to correct me into the proper mode of interpretation—the proper *reality.*

I'm not trying to side with either of these realities in this scenario, but I am trying to point out that it is curious that the opposing viewpoints are formed by those born in separate nations. If the patriots supporting the American forces had been born in the Middle East, into the same conditions as the civilians there, would they support America? Would they have the same convictions, beliefs, and viewpoints? Would they be the *exact people they currently despise?*

Think of how we operate. "The United States is number one! We're blessed to live in the greatest nation in the world!" This innate stance frames an us-versus-them reality. We were born into the "right" situation, whereas others, who are now misled, were born into the "wrong" situation.

There are countless examples of this. Think of opposing sides in wars and how the histories are written in each respective nation. Think of underhanded political tactics, decried as foul by one faction but championed as savvy and necessary by the other faction. Think of gender—would you have the exact same feelings about gender norms and roles if you had lived the experience of another gender?

We easily could be the entire opposite of who we are if our contextual conditions had been different. I'll tie this together with our Anna example from the first chapter. Anna was the student who had a trauma reaction in her classroom and whose emotional states caused challenges in her educational experience. There is a large and loud contingency of people within the United States who advocate the blanket solution of more stern discipline. Their context and perspectives tell them that these children are spoiled, privileged, and do not respect authority; why else would they act this way?

This is a direct example of imposing context. What ground do the people have to imagine this behavior from? Only the ground on which they've stood. If *they themselves* were ever to act that way, they would be bucking authority and only taking into account their own wants.

These people are *self-judging* when projecting their reactions onto a situation of a completely different context. These people *do not understand* Anna's context, needs, emotional state, or reason for acting in such a way. What they do understand is how they, and people like them, respond to rules, structure, and authority. Thus, they posit the answer that is effective for *them*: imposing strict rules. If this happens, people will learn to follow the rules and be disciplined (becoming like them), and the problem will be resolved. This is what I needed; therefore, this is what everyone needs.

People fail to recognize, when evaluating the situation and giving such advice, that *given the proper conditions, they would react just as Anna did*. If they had experienced the exact challenges Anna had, it is highly likely they would have similar emotional responses and challenges in school settings, regardless of discipline. This is why there are trauma-informed approaches and techniques—we are able to see similar patterns of behavior in people who have had adverse experiences. The people simply advocating more discipline are trying to *impose their context and answer* on a person and situation they do not understand.

If someone were to respond to this, "Yeah, but for some of the students, more discipline is the answer!" all that is being said here is, "Don't deny my reality—no matter what you say, my lived experience is real, and my ideas are valid." This response isn't addressing our original concern of what is best for Anna and similar students and is instead a defensive comment meant to reinforce one's beliefs and identity. So, certainly, more discipline and structure are perfect for certain students with certain needs, but the point of that person's comment is entirely self-serving. We do this all the time without having any inkling it's going on and then are flummoxed when others argue with us or don't accept our "valid" advice.

A simpler example of this is literally any news article detailing research. Check the comments section, and you'll see plenty of people brushing off the results as false by sharing their own experience. "Harsher discipline is bad for children? My father whooped my ass, and I turned out just fine. In fact, I learned respect!" All people are doing is saying, "Don't invalidate my reality. This is what I lived through; therefore, this is how things are."

When I am sitting with clients, it is important that I am aware of how much I am imposing my lens, identity, and context upon them. My own lens and context can cloud my ability to truly listen to and help others. My context may encourage me to assert my own opinions, straying the client from *what would be helpful for them*.

If a client, for example, shared an experience about how male supervisors had been rude, dismissive, and sexist to her, what good would it do if I responded, "That hasn't happened in my experience. We can't say all male supervisors are like that."

That is a comically bad response for a therapist to give, but it exemplifies the point well—if I were looking to defend the male portion of my identity over a perceived shaming moment, I would simply be invalidating the client, imposing my reality, and causing serious harm to the therapeutic process. This is why counselors should bring discussions of identity and context into the room, particularly when working with clients of different ethical and cultural backgrounds. Being willing to discuss our lenses as counselors opens the door for clients to feel comfortable expressing and working within their reality without fear it's going to be shut down in the session.

This is what occurs when men deny the reality of women who have faced continued unwanted advances, abuse, and assault. The men are focused on their own reality—they have not seen this occur or may not have done it. They associate their sense of identity with their maleness, and thus the idea that men are doing these things that are wrong is personally troubling to them. They are insecure in their own identity and unwilling to introspect, so the shared reality of women who go through these things is viewed as an "attack." From their insecure perspective, the woman is claiming "all men" are like this. Thus, the women are demeaned, victim-blamed, and made out as if they have ulterior motives. It is easier to deny their reality by warping it than it is to consider the difficult reality that men do these things and cause this suffering. Confronting these things means confronting one's own maleness, which many are unwilling to do.

We often approach social situations without regard for the reality of the other person. We interact with others by attempting to impose our reality. We aren't giving a message of *why don't you just look at it like this?* The real message we're sending is *why can't you just be me?* We are saying, *based on my lived experience and sense of identity, this is what is correct, and you should agree with it.* This is entirely self-serving, and without care, empathy, and a true attempt at connection.

Not all of our innate stances are selfish, however. I'm sure some of you have posed objections related to positions of self-doubt, self-pity, and self-hatred. Some of our most entrenched views about ourselves are these things, rather than impositions of opinion or arrogance. You'll find that, paradoxically, some of the same principles apply here, however. Unfortunately, many times our minds would rather be "right" than be happy, and that includes holding on to and defending negative self-views.

This is something I've had to work with when engaging with the contexts of clients. While we impose our own context and identity, how we conceptualize and develop these things can shift. We have the power to develop our awareness as to what we are doing and why, empowering us to change our thinking and actions. The following chapter illustrates this in two powerful cases, showing that, given the right conditions, we can overcome the barriers of our innate thoughts.

chapter four

Challenging and Reshaping Our Context

I once worked with a student named Larry. He came from a low-income background, had suffered and witnessed past abuse, and had a father who was in jail for a serious crime. Every night Larry went home to a difficult situation: poverty, conflict, and/or household substance abuse. Larry had a difficult time in school. He would be disruptive, making jokes or playing pranks, and would become defensive and argumentative when corrected by a teacher. He'd defend what he was doing and escalate the situation, often going back to the same tactics a few minutes later, making jokes or noises to distract the class.

To teachers, Larry was certainly a challenge, and some thought of him as disruptive, as someone who got enjoyment out of the power struggle. One teacher in particular thought that throwing the book at Larry over and over was the solution—she advocated stern punishment to teach him how he was supposed to act in school. But this wasn't effective with Larry. In fact, his behaviors escalated when such measures were applied.

Eventually, once we had a solid, trusting relationship, Larry admitted to me what was going on. His eyes dropped, I heard a touch of shame in his voice, and I watched him struggle to hold the tears back.

Larry explained to me that he worried about home a lot. He worried about his mother, their finances, his siblings, what would happen when he went home, and most of all his father. These thoughts dominated Larry's thinking—they'd play nonstop on repeat throughout the day during any moment of silence. So what could he do?

Get rid of the silence.

Larry's actions were intended more as a distraction for him than for others. Making jokes and noises and getting into conflict with others *took him away from the torment of his own thoughts.* He admitted that while it was not helpful for his performance in school, he'd rather be in conflict with the teacher than sitting in silence, since conflict was less painful for him.

Larry's actions had natural consequences, however. The teacher's punishment often was isolation from the class, leaving him to stew in his thoughts with an added layer of feeling shame. Other students boxed him out, not wanting to deal with his childish behavior. This temporary relief from his thoughts was becoming a long-term problem, further compounding his challenges.

Larry began to internalize these contextual messages. He thought of himself as "bad" and as a "nuisance" and unable to do well in school. This was despite the fact that he had naturally strong academic abilities. He mentioned that other students could do well—they could overcome the challenges and make it through the day. He expressed that he was just "meant to be nothing."

Larry now thought of himself as "bad" and "incapable." He would defend these viewpoints with evidence, citing experience in the school. This was his lived reality, from which he was operating, but one that was not conducive to his success or happiness. I had to meet Larry where he was at, within his context, if I was going to reach him and help him redefine and rework it.

I validated for Larry that I could understand where he was coming from—that his experience suggested he wasn't doing well and had challenges. Leaning on my relationship with him, however, I challenged Larry's interpretation of the evidence.

"Larry, I know you feel bad about yourself, but let me tell you how I see you. I look at life like a race. We're all running around doing laps on a big track. Some of us are running normally, with nothing on our backs. Some of us, like you, are carrying big backpacks filled with hundred-pound weights. That's the tough stuff with your family and life—not everyone has that. So here you are carrying all that weight, and you're keeping up with and even beating some of the students who don't have anything on their backs. I know you have tough days because of it, but I actually look at you and see a ton of strength."

The look in Larry's eyes changed. There was a flash of realization. A minor epiphany. Here was someone not rejecting his image of self, not rejecting his facts, but instead suggesting a different angle from which to view them. Larry knew I understood where he was coming from due to the hours of conversations we'd had. He trusted I was speaking to him genuinely, and this message got through.

This began a new way in which Larry and I redefined his context. Larry had been down on himself, but he soon was able to say that in his estimation, no one in his class was dealing with even half the things he was. Some of the best-performing students had families that were much more stable, both emotionally as well as financially. I asked Larry if he thought those students would function as well as he was if they were in his situation.

He said they wouldn't, and he was proud of this fact.

Larry's situation was now not only a detriment, but a mark of grit and endurance. He had a bit of a chip on his shoulder, becoming *proud* that he had made it this far in life given his conditions. This pride was a new aspect we instilled in his context by reshaping his thinking, and with this foundation, we were able to make more connections.

Larry and I talked about the strengths and skills he derived from his situation and how these could help him navigate life. We spoke about how he would run his own household, how he would avoid the life problems his family had fallen into, and how his skills would make him capable of handling many work and life challenges. We discussed funding options for higher education, including the military, which he was interested in, giving him a glimpse of a potential future.

Suddenly, now was not forever.

This isn't to say this all made Larry turn things around fully in school. He still had challenges, but he showed noticeable improvement. He could be reached much more frequently when in a bad spot, and he went from completely giving up on school to putting in effort and showing growth. He was making it through because he now had a changed image of himself, his context, and his future.

Part of this is rooted in the counseling theory of cognitive behavioral therapy. Cognitive behavioral therapy, or CBT, is a mainstream counseling approach among the most popular techniques used by mental health professionals today. It is backed by some of the strongest research outcomes in proving client success and maintenance of wellness behaviors.

CBT's main principle can be summarized as this: *Our challenges are not a result of what happens to us, but rather how we think about and act on what has happened to us.* In short, our perspectives, beliefs, and behaviors about life situations are more impactful than the events themselves. This isn't to say that major life events don't impact us or cause major life challenges—rather, the philosophy is that the thinking and patterns of behavior that form after an event are what pose our true challenges and must be addressed. We cannot necessarily change the reality of what occurred, but we can certainly work with the thoughts, beliefs, and behaviors that are causing the stress, depression, or negative behaviors in order to continue forward.

Larry's initial concept was that he was bad, due to how often he was in trouble and how he felt rejected by the teacher and other students. We started working with that automatic belief—that he was bad—in order to make a bridge to possible change, providing an option for a reconceptualization of who he was and why this empowered Larry to consider new thoughts and approaches, which led to changes in behavior.

Similarly, Anna was in my office one day after having a challenge in the classroom. She felt very upset at herself for being in trouble again and was crying on the floor. She blamed herself, labeling herself as "bad" and "wrong." As she cried, she told me that "I'm bad and everyone hates me, and you hate me too!"

This was a child I believed was delightful and talented, lying on the floor mired in a cycle of self-hatred. Rather than try and "save" her from her own emotions with such lines as "No, I don't hate you! You're good!"—which would actually be an attempt to "save" myself from the discomfort of what she was expressing—I put my own feelings aside and met her within her own reality.

Anna was screaming and crying and repeating that she hated herself. I calmly looked at her and said, "Anna, I think you feel really bad about yourself when you get in trouble in the classroom. You feel like you hate yourself, and then because of that, you guess that other people hate you too. I know you hate yourself right now, but that doesn't mean I hate you, and I'm sitting here with you because I care about you."

Anna peeked out at me (as she often did, her keen intellect taking hold) as she made a realization. I had validated what she was going through: Anna did hate herself in that moment. I didn't dismiss it, yet I presented an alternate interpretation of the entire situation. She was imposing her own self-hatred on others, thinking that was the only way others could view her. My interactions with her were direct evidence that I did not hate her, however. Anna calmed down after this statement, and we were able to talk and process what was going on.

This was a powerful moment that would help frame our work together from then on, and it truly helped Anna look at herself and others differently. In my professional opinion, this breakthrough was integral in her incredible success to follow throughout the remainder of the school year.

I bring this up in a clinical sense because it affects us all every day. We all have innate beliefs and automatic assumptions that go unchallenged. We may think good or negative things about ourselves and take this reality for granted. We don't always consider *why* we felt socially awkward or *why* we didn't choose to say anything at that moment. We don't always think about *why* we were angry at that comment or *why* we chose not to pursue that opportunity. Our minds construct a system by which we operate, and our minds are happy to continue working within what they understand. It is comfortable to be defined, yet those definitions are not always helpful, accurate, or set in stone. Larry and Anna "knew" what they were—bad—and were willing to defend it, but upon challenging and reflection, they found much healthier ways to feel about themselves.

Take a moment to reflect on what you think about yourself. Positive, negative, strengths, weaknesses, and what you're meant to accomplish in your life. Why do you think those things? What events have contributed to your self-beliefs?

Next, think about *other ways to interpret or conceptualize these things.* How may an unbiased third party look at you? How do friends, family, and others conceptualize these things as related to you? Is it helpful or healthy to continue thinking about some of these things in the way you do? What could you work on? How could you challenge yourself? What are some beliefs and behaviors that may need to change?

We have a tough time doing this due to self-judgment and shame, which sneak in when we critically analyze ourselves. Shame is something we will avoid at all costs. Our minds are built to feel correct and to maintain what we believe. We don't want to feel blamed or wrong or part of any bad thing in the world. We'll get into how this plays out later, but for now note that people will viciously fight with others and do mental gymnastics to justify their actions, all to avoid feeling shame. This is because, even when we make mistakes, our innate reaction is to go, *This is why my reaction is valid and makes sense. My experience makes this reasonable, and people in my situation would also do this.* Our mind fights for our reality, our innate stance, to avoid the pain of shame, even though recognition of ourselves being incorrect at something can be a major step in growing and becoming happier.

A quick note—supplementary reading to this book, as well as simply incredible reads on their own, are the books by Dr. Brené Brown, including *The Gifts of Imperfection.* Her work on shame and how it impacts us in our daily lives is incredible, and I neglected to go in-depth on shame within this work due to viewing it as a disservice to her masterful portrayal.

So critical to our shame responses are the automatic thoughts, such as *This is just how I am.* You'll hear people say this in defense of behaviors or beliefs. "It's just how I am—I've always been this way." This is a rejection of our own freedom to change. This is avoidance of searching for new modes of operation and shying away from the challenge. We all do this, but recognizing when we are doing it is essential if we are going to change and improve the quality of our lives.

I often advise counselors-in-training to look out for these lines. "It's just how I am" or "I've always been this way" show a client hasn't critically examined a portion of their personality or life. I encourage the counselor-in-training to ask questions about this behavior. When does the client first remember it? How has it changed? What has impacted it? How has it shifted as they've gotten older? Does anyone in their family have the same trait? Where do they think it came from? This opens the client to realizing that many aspects to our perspective and behaviors are *not innate* and that they can reconceptualize themselves. So much of who we are comes from our contexts, our families, our experiences—if we just brush this off, we're denying our chance to reshape and remold our identities and lives.

Who we are is not innate, though our minds try to look at the world this way. An ever-shifting world, with changing beliefs, values, and moral systems is uncomfortable for our minds to process. Our minds sense we can't control all of this change, and thus we feel anxious and unsafe. We often try to avoid these things, using "facts" to justify our beliefs about self and the world, remaining rigid in our stances even when they are harmful.

When we are children, we seek out concrete truths in the world. We want to know what is right and wrong. We want to understand fairness and impose it in every single interaction. Where do we get these conceptions from? Morality and manners and beliefs come from home and school through the stories we are told. These moral lessons are often parables—simple and direct. They make the world seem simple and straightforward, rooted in a sense of right and wrong. The one kid at school yells back at the teacher—they are wrong, they are flawed. This is a comfortable and simple interpretation of reality. However, as we get older, we may realize that that child was abused and wasn't receiving the love they needed at home or school. Now the world seems less black and white. Morality becomes more ambiguous, with situations showing us there isn't always a clear right and wrong. Rather than embrace this and contemplate what this means for who we are in the world, it is much more comfortable to dig into our childhood definitions and continue imposing them on the external world.

As a child, I believed adults had power and were competent. I thought those in authority positions had earned them. The older I became, however, I saw how circumstances contributed to so much of the world, and many people in charge of things (think of your least favorite politicians) did not seem intelligent or competent at all. I had been taught that leadership was obtained through merit and effort—not through nepotism, networking, or chance. I could remain walled up to the views I had in childhood and cherry-pick facts and representations to claim these views to still be an overarching reality. I could also be willing to reconsider my worldview, my moral system, what resonates with my identity, and how I now must reinterpret the world around me. If I'm unwilling to take this second step, I'm choosing to only engage with the world as the creation I've made it out to be rather than dealing with it as it actually exists.

If we want to have healthier relationships with ourselves and others, we must first come to a deeper understanding of who we are and what motivates us. This includes considering our identity, context, perspectives, behaviors, and what contributes to these things and why. It includes critically analyzing our thoughts and behaviors and being willing to take feedback from ourselves and others. This is not easy to do, of course, but I'll provide some tips below.

Daily journaling is an excellent way to express the underlying thoughts and emotions we experience every day. Structured journaling, where we intentionally list our thoughts and feelings about particular issues or goals, allows us to tangibly see and analyze what we are going through. For example, if I feel anxiety daily, maybe my journal focuses around my feelings before, during, and after my anxiety moments in a day. Let's look at what I was thinking. Is there anything I can change or something I haven't looked at fully? Journaling can take many forms and be creative as well. I actually suggest you do online searches about journaling, both therapeutic and nontherapeutic, in order to decide which method and approach fits best for you.

Mindfulness is a term for self-awareness of what is occurring between the mind and the body. There are countless mindfulness exercises intended to ground an individual in the moment—to help them understand what is immediately occurring in the mind and body. Mindfulness and grounding exercises range from deep mindful breathing (to calm and balance the self) to counting exercises to guided meditation and yoga. Mindfulness techniques have a main goal of pulling one's mind away from the *noise*—whatever stressors, anxieties, or distractions are making it difficult to understand the self and the moment. By putting the body in a calm, relaxed state and focusing on the immediate, we can hear thoughts that were drowned out, or be empowered to clearly think and analyze current situations. Mindfulness exercises are helpful as both a preventative and reactive measure, done both as a daily routine and in response to stressors. Similar to journaling, I encourage you to search for mindfulness activities and resources as a tool to add to your self-awareness toolbox.

Another way to do this is by practicing *healthy self-doubt*. This is a term I've used in my personal life, though it may exist somewhere as an academic or psychological concept. By this term I mean *critically analyzing one's own reactions, thoughts, and desires without detrimental self-judgment*. Doubting one's self should not automatically mean feeling bad about one's self or abandoning one's principles. Rather, we can go into situations with some skepticism regarding our own motives.

Questions such as "Why am I in such a bad mood?" or "What is making me feel off today?" or "Was it really necessary for me to say that?" empower us to examine what is going on with our thinking and emotions. Self check-ins allow for reflective moments where we can consider the impact of our actions.

I've found, personally, that this has helped with responsibility to myself and others. Sometimes I get an impulse to splurge on an unhealthy lunch, or during a conversation, I get a sudden rush to share a story about myself. I pause mentally to ask myself whether these things are necessary and where the urges are coming from. What other piece of my day, either before or recently, was lacking and made me feel the need to do this? Before I snap at someone for "bugging me,"

I pause to ask if they really are, or if my emotional state has me in a place where I am interpreting their normal interaction as a threat.

This self-reflective check-in does require some self-doubt. I'm not always "right" in what I want or what I think about others. This doubt does not have to be destructive but rather can be constructive. Imagine these reflective moments as workouts—it hurts to do a good workout, but the actions contribute to us becoming happier, healthier, and more capable.

In general, a willingness to elicit and accept feedback also assists in understanding how we impose our contexts and why. In-depth conversations with friends, family, and loved ones can help provide an understanding of how your context translates. How do others make meaning of how you think and act? Rather than becoming defensive and *denying their interpretation*, openness is key. We need to be willing to accept that *how we come off is valid in their interpretation*. This allows us more self-understanding and potential for any changes we desire.

A major step in increased self-awareness is attending counseling. Contrary to popular belief, counseling is intended to be *preventative*. Most common conceptions of counseling are *reactive*; people attend only when they have "major" issues. Counseling is great for higher-level issues but is also designed as a place for a person to explore their life, wants, and needs. It is designed to be a space to work on positive growth regardless of the severity level. Since a counselor is an empathetic, impartial observer, counseling provides a unique opportunity to explore ideas and feelings that are difficult to bring up to those close to us in life. In counseling, we can say it like it is, and the counselor will be there to help us every step of the way. My most successful experiences as a client in counseling have been the times I've elected to go when there was no major presenting issue—being in a stable space allowed me to really explore and work on deeper aspects of my personality and life.

I understand, given the cost of counseling and insurance protocols, that attending is difficult. There are voices in the field moving toward greater access, and over time I have faith that they will win out as the cultural attitude toward mental health and wellness progresses in this country. If attainable, however, I encourage you to prioritize this as a resource; wellness is paramount in our daily functioning.

Self-awareness and check-ins are concepts that seem simple enough to understand, but as our own contexts, identity, and level of awareness change, these things morph and take on deeper forms. Often, the more we become aware, the more we realize just how little we had previously been aware of! This creates more for us to think about, reflect, and work on—which may seem daunting but eventually builds on itself in a fruitful way.

For this reason, this book will progress by encouraging an exploration of your context and those you see in the world around you. In order to facilitate your own awareness, I hope to empower you to see how these things play out and why. Each of the following chapters will get into the impact of context across different aspects of identity and interaction.

chapter five

Social Media and Politics in Context

I magine there was a device that allowed you to represent yourself to anyone instantly in any way you desire. You could represent your thoughts, feelings, and physical appearance in the most favorable manner; instantly express yourself; and connect with others who are like-minded. In fact, if you were ever challenged on your beliefs and biases, you could instantly find countless sources proving your viewpoint correct and disparaging the ideas of anyone different from you. This device would allow you to feel a sense of power in determining what sources of information were correct and what deserves to be shared with others, and allow you to judge others based on small amounts of information interpreted quickly and efficiently. The world, once so complex and overwhelming, is now in the palm of your hand, with you in complete control of how you are represented to the world and how the world is represented to you.

What impact would that device have on people?

Would people be more likely to listen to others, critically examine their biases, and connect with new sources of information? Would people potentially use this device to avoid introspection and taking responsibility? Would they falsely represent themselves for a spike in their ego? Would they admonish and put others down for the sake of feeling superior to someone else? Would they cherry-pick information for the sake of maintaining this created version of self, newly formed sense of community, and distraction from their insecurities?

Smartphones and social media have taken the world by storm. Across a single decade, they have gone from novelties to staples of American culture and identity. If one desires, they can use social media to receive news that is tailored to their biases and viewpoints. They may block accounts and ideas that counter their views, receive a steady feed of information that seemingly reinforces their stances and constructed identities, and receive support for treating those who think differently in a cruel and dismissive manner. The social community is no longer limited to the local sphere—one can now represent thought, ideal, and identity and receive significant interaction virtually. This can be done whether or not the information being shared (about the individual or the world) is true, and in fact, this rarely matters.

Truth is rarely the point.

And why would it be? If one can feel connected, supported, popular, and loved through this medium, why would they seek to undo the position they've established? Why would they critically evaluate their biases and flaws? It is much easier to use a tool to quickly justify how one is representing one's self and/or mistreating others. If we can prove others are bad and less than ourselves, we can seem to be "right" while they are "wrong," similar to the hard-line worldviews we establish as children.

What an escape from the complexities of the world.

This escape is both profitable and addicting. It is designed to increase ad revenue. Psychologists are regularly consulted on the construction of social media apps. What will allow for a quick release of dopamine? What will make someone anxious for information so they continually check back? What type of products are most likely to be bought by people associated with these online groups and trends? While the major companies make money, the rest of us bicker and disparage, falling further from ourselves and others.

I worked with a child client once who looked hopelessly at the floor and told me that the one thing he wanted most in life was for his parents to look at their phones less and pay attention to him more. At eight years old, he felt that they cared much more about what was going on within those devices than they did for him. When he would ask them to play, they would often be short and snap at him, letting him know they were busy. A world they could control and interact with more easily was more appealing to them than the work of being a parent. The need to continue to get a rush from interaction had effectively robbed a child of the full attention of his parents. It was no surprise that this boy desperately sought the attention of adults in the school and would cry if they focused more highly on other students. His parents had adapted to an online reality, leaving him without what he needed in his everyday reality. Warmth, genuine care, and attention were needed to help this little guy process what he thought about himself, his family, and others in the world around him.

Teens I worked with reported intense anxiety related to their social media use. It would be difficult to log off at night when there were so many more messages to read or videos to watch. There was more information, more opinions, and more things that their friends had shared. If they didn't engage in these behaviors, they would lose friends in real life as well. Keeping up with the rush of information and posting content became expected, a mark of teenage culture. Many were concerned with being entertaining, funny, or informative, rather than being authentic or connecting. The popularity contest many of us go through as teens has now been streamlined virtually, ever present and ever demanding.

Studies consistently demonstrate that social media use strongly correlates with rising levels of anxiety, depression, and self-harm in teenage populations. And is this any surprise? If your mind begins developing an addiction to a device that allows you to constantly compare yourself to others on an application where you are often fighting or being put down, what will happen? If these same platforms overemphasize contentious and tragic news because they get more clicks within their profit model, what might a developing adult feel about the world and the potential for hope moving forward? If families sit in restaurants each focused on their own virtual reality instead of communicating with one another and spending quality time, how much do the members know and support each other? How much structure is available for confused and anxious teens?

Social media truly allows for the social construction of an individual reality. The problem with this is that an individual construction of reality prevents someone from truly getting what they need in order to grow and be successful. Social media allows us to feel temporary validation at the expense of long-term self-examination and connectedness. We have a quick fix community to associate with, feel accepted by, and all the evidence in the world to "prove" we are "right" and these online profiles are "our people." Think of it as eating an ice cream sundae for every meal. Temporarily, this is exciting and delicious! In the long run, however, it would have devastating consequences for health, well-being, and mood.

We're being sold our own version of truth. The result is that we distrust and hate one another, feel more anxious and depressed, and become more dependent on media to keep us "informed" and "safe." We have a difficult time abandoning our sources because they make us feel "right," "safe," and "informed," even though they are contributing to our anxiety, depression, and disconnection from others in everyday life.

I worked with a college client, Jeff, who was dealing with stress related to social media identity and political viewpoints. Jeff, who identified as conservative, put a lot of stock in his online posting and community interactions. Jeff found, however, that he felt isolated in real life at college, and any knowledge of his political views and occasional extreme posts made him feel ostracized. Jeff hadn't been successful in developing in-person relationships throughout his life and struggled academically in college. He had not always been attracted to more extreme conservative groups but found himself pulled in online through videos and forum communities.

What was going on here? As a counselor, I had to offer Jeff warmth and compassion every single step of the way. I was curious as to what he thought and why. What was important to him politically? Personally? Socially? What would an ideal college and life experience look like? How could we get him there? If I had instead started by confronting Jeff about the fiery nature and cruel content of some of his posts, I would have appeared to Jeff to be another person he could not connect with, furthering his dive into this virtual reality.

By providing Jeff compassion and acting with curiosity, I learned that Jeff had low self-esteem. He had always dreamed of accomplishing more and felt as if he had let his family down. He had a difficult relationship with his father, who was an alcoholic and would beat members of the family, and a big reason he had moved toward right-wing political philosophies was that he felt that the struggles of men like him were not represented in media or education. In short, Jeff felt alone and left out, since socially he was awkward and unable to share his story and the pains of his experience weren't often present in media narratives.

It's important to consider what is going on in this scenario. Jeff feels pain about who he is and what he has gone through. He is unable to connect with others in a way that satisfies him. He feels anxiety, depression, and finally anger about this. An online source allows him to get information to turn those feelings around and take them out on others instead of himself. The online sources tell him that society is to blame for leaving him out, that media narratives exclude White men like him as part of a conspiracy, that he is actually smart and capable for seeing through the plans, and that those who disagree with him are ignorant and full of hatred. Suddenly, the man who felt weak, incapable, and alone can feel informed, powerful, and together. Unfortunately, the vessels by which this occur include Jeff lashing out at those who are different from him. While this allows Jeff to connect with an online community, he finds that his day-to-day life interactions are becoming more stressful, with him feeling more anxiety and uncomfortable levels of anger.

These media sources often included promotion of conspiracy theories. These theories were comfortable in the sense that they assured Jeff and others that they were in the know. He wasn't a failure—he was insightful. As long as he believed and followed, he'd have community, he'd have identity, and he'd have purpose in a world that previously had seemed void of it. It's critical to consider how these conditions came to be.

Online media sources and influencers sell the products of community and identity. Many of these influencers and media figures spout ideas that are controversial or intentionally ignorant to spark debates and get shares for the sake of profitability. By misrepresenting groups of people, the poster shows how ignorant and evil the other side is, their rageful responses prove that these are bad people, and thus it is imperative for people to follow this social media figure. This provides up-to-date information as well as evidence to confirm the viewer's sense of identity and community. This is the product being sold through deceptive and manipulative means, with all of us as the consumer taking it in to greatly harmful effect.

To reach Jeff, I had to understand Jeff and provide support. While I personally thought much of what he was posting was hateful and harmful to the world, the way to allow him to grow past these habits and beliefs was through empathy, not hatred. Online, Jeff received hatred from those who thought differently than him, which convinced him that they were indeed bad people and further solidified his connection to these conspiracy communities. Those reaching out with opposing viewpoints were doing so to put him down and feel superior to him, causing him anger and shame, pushing him further away from any helpful information those people could provide.

When our conversations shifted to how Jeff felt about himself, progress was made. We were able to connect his anxiety and self-esteem to how he behaved online. We were able to imagine a healthier way of functioning and connecting with students on campus. Jeff was able to verbalize how he'd been "hooked" into the social media game. After he had been listened to, cared about, and supported, Jeff was willing to be challenged and consider new ways to look at the world around him. And indeed, as Jeff tried to join clubs and activities on campus, exposing himself more directly to those different from him, his views became less extreme and he became much more comfortable with himself and others.

The new mode of communication through online sources has stoked the intense political polarization pulling our nation apart. No longer are there simple disagreements, but rather outright hatred. This makes sense, since social media allows identities to fight other identities directly. It is not about opinions or principles, but instead about people feeling known, heard, cared about, and represented. Part of that occurs by believing other groups of people (misrepresented by these media sources) are outright evil. Under this model, it makes complete sense that people's trust in others who are different politically is at an all-time low.

If someone shares a political viewpoint on social media that we disagree with, our minds link it to the other terrible things we've seen on social media even tangentially related to the topic. Thus, this person is now associated with the worst of the worst, either unaware or part of the bad team, and we knowingly or unknowingly react to this. This detached form of interaction doesn't allow for in-depth sharing or connection but rather encourages quick associations of how others are wrong or different.

Within these venues, people tend to engage in political discourse as if the other person is not human. They come from an innate stance that the other is misinformed, ignorant, or outright evil. This creates conflict and frustration, with no real sense of accomplishment at the end. It is a jockeying for position, an attempt to get a slam dunk on someone and feel superior. Even if one is coming from a better, more thoughtfully informed political viewpoint, if their motivation is to shame another and gain recognition for this, they are not doing good. They are looking to put another down and boost their own image—using more enlightened information to do this doesn't excuse the selfish and negative urges. Individuals on every point of the political spectrum engage in this behavior, causing us to mistrust and dislike one another more day by day.

When we choose to engage in political conversations online, what are we getting from it? Are we approaching this situation truly hoping to help enlighten and inform someone? Are we entering in good faith hoping to share information and perspectives and develop a connection? Are we instead looking to prove another wrong so we feel better about ourselves and justified in our preconceptions?

How healthy is your own personal social media use? Does it help you learn more about yourself and others in a positive manner that prepares you for the challenges of your day-to-day life? How do you feel about the nature of the conversations you hold over these platforms? How do you feel about the news stories you receive? Are the headlines crafted in a certain way? Is there a certain percentage of the stories you see that are negative or spun to emphasize negative aspects?

This isn't to say we shouldn't fight problematic views, that we shouldn't fight for what is right or stand up for others. What this is saying is that we often aren't evaluating why we are engaging in these conversations, checking whether we are making that sort of progress, or putting ourselves in a position to truly make the differences we wish to. Instead, we are often becoming overwhelmed with negativity, to the point where it breeds anxiety and depression within us. This anxiety and depression prevents us from being our best selves and accomplishing what we truly wish we could.

I've worked with several clients who identified their source of anxiety and depression to be the state of the world. Global warming, racism, war, wage inequality, sexual assault—how could one be happy when all these threats are so pervasive and imminent? How could one not obsess about these daunting realities that threaten the very future of society? Through social media, their minds are overloaded with stories and images of injustice, suffering, and impending doom.

A metaphor to consider, borrowed from Confucius, is the idea that "the man who moves a mountain does so one stone at a time." If we stare at a mountain and consider trying to move all of it at once, we are overwhelmed with despair, paralyzed by the futility of the effort. However, if we avoid the challenges of the entire world and consider what we must accomplish to be positive in the day to day, eventually tangible progress is made.

I've noticed that clients who are overwhelmed by the state of the world are thinking about "the mountain" all at once. They are considering all the dangers and threats in the world and find themselves feeling hopeless. What they are not often considering are the individual daily steps they can take to combat their anxiety and make tangible differences in the issues that concern them.

If a client is immersing themselves in media, finding more and more reason to support their worries, it's understandable why this anxiety is so strong. Some will contend that the anxiety is valid and should be there. Is it helpful to be overwhelmed and paralyzed by the information we come across? Is it helpful to seek this information out?

Often, people say that there is no other way to take it. This is an example of anxiety and worry justifying their own existence. My question to clients is this: What do they have to do in order to be their best, most happy selves? This is crucial not only for its own sake, but also for the sake of making a difference in major issues in the world. If we are wrought with anxiety and depression, we're unlikely to be standing on a solid foundation. Without a solid foundation, it's unlikely we are doing our very best to change the world in a positive way.

We're so eager to impose our opinion and wants upon the world. We want things to change and life to be what we'd like it to be. The problem with media and political discourse is that we are bombarded with images and ideas that show us the world isn't what we'd like it to be. Instead of feeling angry and defeated by this, we can improve ourselves and the world step by step. Instead of feeling isolated and hopeless about the projected state of the external world, we can instead build a solid foundation within our internal world to deal with any future life challenges.

"Be the change you wish to see in the world," as Gandhi said. Or as a proverb goes, "A journey of a million miles begins with a single step." If we take care of ourselves, see the positives in ourselves and the world, look for the good people and helpers, we can make a tangible difference. We can choose to focus on our strengths and what inspires us. We can use these things to counter the negatives in the world. Consumption of media and political arguments that results in us becoming cynical, anxious, depressed, and inactive only entrench us in our own biases—that others are bad and there's no hope—instead of empowering us to learn, grow, and make a difference.

Consider how your identity is related to social media use and your political views. If your online accounts disappeared today, how would you feel? What would change about who you are? How you view yourself? What do these answers mean? Do you think your anxiety and depression would rise or fall if you disengaged from social media usage? What would this look or feel like?

What particular facts or life experiences have shaped your political worldview? How have the direct experiences of those different from you shaped your political worldview? How early on in life do you recall developing a political worldview? What factors internalized or changed it?

How can you take pauses from the constant information barrage to get in touch with your mood and feelings? How can facing these things allow you to be balanced and calm when talking to those who are different? How can you seek to learn, grow, and connect?

Critically analyze your thoughts and feelings in your mind and body the next time you log on to social media. Evaluate your automatic thoughts when you read something politically concerning to you. What is going on? Why? How is it helpful or not? What do you do with this new information? Perhaps you could sit down and journal out these feelings. What thoughts do you notice? How accurate are these reactions to the state of your own individual life?

We consume information passively through social media, when often it is having an active effect on our emotions. Mindfulness while consuming media of all forms is key—what biases are these sources appealing to? What anxieties are being provoked? Is this helpful in me growing to be a better person? How can I limit my use and find more time for inward reflection instead of outward distraction? How can I spread more kindness to those I know and others in the world? By focusing on these questions, posting them on notes throughout the house, or making lists of action steps to take to answer them, we can live more presently. When in tune with our minds and bodies, we are more empowered to recognize and process our own feelings, putting us in the best position to meet others where they are at and foster positive connections.

chapter six

Context and Identity Within Social Class

After the death of my father, our family of three was living on about $15,000 a year in income. In a rural area, there aren't many jobs, and finding one that paid above the minimum wage of $7.25 was difficult. I drove my beat-up '95 Honda Civic about 30 minutes one way to work at Kmart for minimum wage while I worked on finishing my bachelor's and master's degrees. A portion of my student loan debt was used to pay the mortgage to make sure my family had a roof over our heads.

My mother worked various jobs, such as a maid at a local inn, a cashier, and a deli worker. None of the jobs provided much in the way of income or advancement. My brother was in and out of employment, not having a vehicle of his own to provide transportation. Without public transportation options, this was a major detriment.

I'd commute 35 miles to the University of Scranton for my schooling. It was a lovely institution, but it was also a small, private liberal arts college. This meant the price tag was well above anything we could conceivably afford, but luckily I was offered significant enough scholarships and just enough loans to make it work.

The price tag of the university attracted people from a social class I hadn't yet encountered. Back home, the *teachers* were looked at as the well-to-do. People were *envious* of their high starting salaries. If one didn't own one of the few successful local businesses, work at the school, or work at the hospital, they didn't have too much of anything financially. I was exposed to a much different social reality at my university, however, where teachers would be far from those at the highest reaches.

This came to mind most saliently for me one morning while I was in line to get a breakfast sandwich. I'd scraped together some spare bills and change for a little treat to start my long day of classes. I stood in the food court and was second in line, behind another student, who spoke to the man preparing the sandwiches.

He was an older gentleman. I'd seen him plenty of times before, tending the grill for breakfast or lunch. I thought of him as "the sausage flipper" in my mind, since so often I saw him doing just that. He lived up to his moniker as he greeted the student in front of me with a smile. This was right after Easter, and he asked her how she'd been and what she did over break.

The student was pleasant, greeting him with a smile and informing him she was well. She mentioned, in a tone that seemed genuine, that they really didn't do all too much, just spent some leisurely downtime at their vacation house, which was on some island off the coast of Florida.

I remember the feeling I got when I heard those words. It was a sinking feeling, as if I was falling into an abyss at the center of myself. A *collapsing* feeling—all the energy I had summoned to start the day was suddenly tapped.

Before my father passed, he had a stroke. He'd been in and out of the hospital so much that we no longer could afford calling an ambulance. I recall vividly having to cradle my father like a child, holding him close, as I carried him to the car so we could get to the hospital.

This was my normal.

After he passed, the financial issues worsened, in conjunction with the emotional suffering my family endured. We were in constant threat of losing our home. The Honda Civic I drove had to be purchased with student loans, since my '98 Toyota Camry had finally kicked the bucket. My mother was working any hour she could to put food on the table and throw the occasional help to me for gas money. My friends back home always wanted to go out to eat for 35-cent wing night, but I had to tell them I couldn't afford it. I still get teary thinking about how many times they paid for me just so I could come and have some fun.

I worked at Kmart, doing what I could, but I never had any money. There wasn't time for trips or adventures. My break had been spent at home, in a sullen, depressing atmosphere, working on school assignments and worrying about the uncertain future. I couldn't *imagine* having a beach house and getting to relax in it. I couldn't *fathom* saying that "I didn't do all that much" after traveling to a beach house.

How could she say that? How the hell could she make that out to be no big deal? That's extravagant. That's a dream. That's something next to no people get to experience!

These were my thoughts, which got even worse after I heard the sausage flipper's reply.

"Oh, I love that place. My wife and I have a house down there too!"

The grill master in the food court gets a beach house too. I get a difficult home situation, mounting student loan debt, and depression. I considered leaving the line and abandoning my breakfast sandwich. I was being wasteful splurging on it anyway.

Why was I even trying? I didn't belong here. No matter how hard I grinded, there was just more pain, the specter of poverty hanging over my head. I should just quit school, get out while my debt was somewhat manageable, and find whatever full-time job I could to keep a roof over our heads. Getting out just wasn't in the cards for me.

This excerpt, from one of my works of fiction, describes what I was going through well:

> Every day is just that never-ending cycle. Surviving it is enough. Who can plan? Who can prepare? And since fate tends to show that any bit of savings you have is soon to evaporate, why not treat yourself in the moment? Why not buy a sandwich or a candy bar to make the day slightly less oppressive? Sure, you can't afford it, but you know you can't really afford anything. Why not feel like a normal person? Seriously, treating yourself to a Diet Coke feels like a moment of control in a life that's spiraled out of it. You don't know if you'll always be able to afford the damn rent, but you usually do have enough spare change for that Coke, and there's no real feeling like that moment of victory.

I'm glad I didn't run from that moment of victory. I stayed in line and got the breakfast sandwich. I gutted it out through the day and stuck with my education. I eventually got out of the difficult situation, but that context and those experiences have shaped my context and how I look at the world.

Originally, I felt cynical and upset at the student in front of me. I thought she was out of touch. Insensitive. Ungrateful. I thought she utterly lacked perspective. From my context, she did—she was unaware of entire facets of my reality. However, as I've grown older, I've realized that I was out of touch and unaware.

I don't doubt she was being genuine in her sentiments. She likely didn't believe it was a very big deal due to her own life experiences with travel and vacation, or perhaps those of others. Undoubtedly, I imagine she had friends from the university and back home who'd had more extravagant adventures over break. Perhaps they owned multiple vacation homes or went across the world on a mini adventure. Perhaps she was at the lower end of the socioeconomic status of her community.

Now, for years this concept would anger me. How could entire swaths of our nation be so out of touch? So in their own bubbles as to not recognize their overt privilege? But let me not cast stones while living in a glass house myself.

How could I consider my life situation as being one of poverty?

Sure, we were below the poverty line for a family of three. Certainly, we had challenges with the mortgage. And yes, our vehicles were shakily reliable at best. But we did have cell phones. I had a smartphone, in fact. I also had multiple video game systems. I did, in fact, have a car, and our home had electricity, including heating and air-conditioning. We had cable and internet, and were within driving distance of restaurants and entertainment such as movie theaters.

Imagine if I traveled to a more desolate area of the United States or another nation more beset with poverty. Imagine a truly poverty-stricken area—an actual lack of access to food and clean drinking water, no electricity or stable housing, no access to entertainment options. These people are truly *struggling to survive*. There are millions upon millions of people in this world in *true desolate situations*.

Imagine if I complained to those people about my poverty.

How do you think they would view me?

As out of touch? Insensitive? Unaware and unappreciative of my privileges?

It's curious for me to think how, based on my context, I looked upward and placed judgment on another, when based on the context of others, I fit those same definitions. Depending on where we are looking from and what we have lived through, poverty and privilege look quite different.

This is not to deny the pain and suffering of poverty. It is real, and painful, and has effects—but the realization that my thoughts and perspectives were as malleable to context as anyone else's helped me make profound realizations about how we view and treat each other based on our socioeconomic backgrounds. The anger I felt was not helpful—it was borne out of my own suffering and only made it continue. My reaction to that situation alienated me from another person and from myself.

I have a friend who grew up in a neighborhood where the average income put just about everyone in town in the top 10% of households in the United States. It's a beautiful neighborhood, with a lovely community and school system, and access to shopping and entertainment. It's the type of place one would be incredibly advantaged to grow up in.

His family was near the bottom end of means in this community. Thus, while they were doing well in the context of the United States, compared to other families in the community, they weren't as well off. My friend *saw* and *felt* this as he was growing up, becoming concerned that his family was not doing well. They did not have the multiple households, beach houses, or money to fly to Europe on a whim. While their house was worth a considerable amount, it paled in comparison to the multimillion-dollar homes in the community.

My friend wondered if his family was well off financially. He thought of his upbringing as squarely middle class. This is despite the fact that he grew up within the top 10% of incomes in the United States. Should we blame him for this? Make him feel out of touch? Give him examples of our own financial pain to illustrate how wrong he was?

Who is that for? The benefit of that person? Society? Is it intended to constructively make things better? Or do we want our reality validated, our wrath felt, and someone to take it out on? Because even when we are right about things (in this case, poverty being a huge, worldwide issue), we must consider our motives and whether we are trying to positively change things.

We instead tend to impose our contexts on others. When we force our reality down their throats, we create shame and push them away from us and our ideas. Even if our ideas are valuable and have validity, if we deliver them in this vicious way, they will not be received by others. We often dishonor our own great ideas by presenting them from a hurt and insecure position, trying to shame another instead of trying to help them learn and grow.

My friend is a thoughtful, caring, and empathetic person who has been generous and helpful to me on so many occasions. He is willing to be challenged and to reconceptualize his upbringing and sense of socioeconomic status. There was no reason for me to put him down, make him feel stupid, or make him feel ashamed of a situation he never chose. Could we have valuable conversations that could enlighten the two of us about the reality of poverty in the United States and what that means? Absolutely.

And I can never forget one thing: I would have some of the EXACT perceptions my friend has if I had been raised in his sociocultural situation. If I was to better my relationships, outlook, and personal wellness, I had to work on what I could: *challenging and reshaping my own beliefs about social class by understanding my own contextual experiences and limitations.*

You'll see news headlines crafted to get your attention regarding this. I saw one akin to "Is making $250,000 a year really considered well-off?" These stories are crafted this way because those writing them know they will get attention. People jump at the chance to impose their context and share their personal facts. This is the type of story that can be disproved by countless of our lives—so it will get comments and shares. We are all so ready to explain how out of touch anyone who has that viewpoint is, with our lived experiences as prime examples as to why. We are so desperate to have our realities heard and validated that we constantly fall into media marketing traps.

If I were aggressive and judgmental to my friend, it's possible that he would be turned off to hearing me out about social class. He might think that people of a lower social class are judgmental or envious. He might feel personally attacked and move away from a deeper level of connection and understanding.

Instead, both of us approached each other with open minds and hearts, willing to let the other express their social context. This helped us teach each other as well as helped each of us to explore and examine our privileges and biases. We had a positive impact on one another—allowing each of us to be less ingrained in our own context and less out of touch with the reality of another. From the poor man's context, where money is the fabled solution to all woes, I was shocked to hear about some of the unsavory aspects of his home community and its social norms. It turns out the grass isn't always greener on the other side, and I was using one facet of life to judge an entire segment of people and the validity of their worldviews.

I'll flip this around to an example regarding people from a higher socioeconomic class judging those in a lower class.

We often hear the judgments regarding the poor blared over media and written in books. These claims place the burden of poverty on the individual, as if it is some personal or moral failing that has resulted in their situation. Why don't they just work harder? Why don't they get training or an education? How come they can afford a phone if they're so poor? Why would they pick a useless college degree if they didn't want debt?

These viewpoints often come from the context of those with privilege. They are essentially saying, "Given the life that I have lived, I would have to have screwed up majorly to end up in that situation. I would have to have been lazy, wasted money, or ignored easy-to-follow advice."

These last bits may be true, if they were to end up in an impoverished situation. What this fails to take into account is how others *do not have the same access to privileges, assistance, knowledge, and information, and that not all of these things are applicable to other peoples' contexts.*

Let's take a general example, a profile of no student in particular but one that has many general qualities of the students I worked with as a counselor.

This student was raised in poverty. He knows of financial spending habits only what he has learned from his parents, which includes spending money as soon as you get it and using credit cards as a way to get the necessities when needed. No one in his family has ever held a professional job, and both parents work part-time with no benefits. The idea of career development and progression is foreign. Neither parent understands how college works, can help with the application process, or understands how to do the financial aid paperwork necessary for a college application. The student knows next to nothing about college, majors, career choices, or how to do these things without his parents' guidance. He also doesn't know how important these things really are, since they are not discussed. There is no college fund, there is no car provided when he is old enough to drive, there is no real talk of the future, since scrapping by in the present isn't guaranteed. The school system has limited career education, and the topic seems foreign to him. Any institution of higher education is multiple hours away and seems to be a different world. There's no education about financial planning for college, including student loan details. A lot of the emphasis at his high school is on finding a major and career that a student loves. The student is soon graduating high school. Here are the student's options:

1. Get a job locally, which will pay a poverty wage and offer little advancement. The factory jobs that were once a staple of the local economy are gone, and the biggest employer jobs-wise is corporate retail. No matter how hard the person works, it is unlikely there will be a job opportunity that will get him well beyond the reaches of poverty.

2. Get a job in another area, which requires money to move and secure an apartment, which the student does not have. This also requires knowledge, experience, and guidance the student does not have due to a lack of support from home. The student also doesn't really know what jobs would pay well and how to pursue them. No one has ever taught the student about a resume.

3. Go to college and incur major debt with the hope to get a career based on a major he enjoys. The student has no sense of what an internship is or what a career services office is. The student believes that getting a college degree means they will get a job.

Are any of these solid options? The student was born into a context that did not provide education or guidance about careers, training, and financial planning. As humans, we typically go with the support and advice we are provided by those we trust—friends, family, and school— but what if these sources are based on a context of poverty themselves? What type of quality information and guidance are we receiving to break the cycle and end up in a better socioeconomic situation?

And let's not forget—there is zero room for error in this student's situation. He literally cannot afford to take an extra semester if he wants to switch majors. If he moves to a new area and ends up out of a job for whatever reason, that may mean homelessness. The silly mistakes so many people make in their late teens and early 20s mean complete devastation to someone in a low socioeconomic situation. Let's also not forget that *many of these people are relied on to help their parents survive.*

Multiple research studies show that the highest predictor of life income is the class one is born into. This holds even when individuals of lower classes demonstrate higher skills or achieve higher levels of education. Stability in economics and home culture provides knowledge of how to access certain jobs, networking opportunities to get those jobs, and a safety net that encourages an expansion of money-making activities beyond a standard job. Individuals in these situations are also more familiar with the concepts of professionalism, the culture of higher education, and the process of how to access support systems within academia. This set of allowances puts individuals of a high socioeconomic status at a major advantage in succeeding. While an individual of a lower socioeconomic status can be successful, a minor misstep may undo their entire effort, since there may be virtually no support system in place.

I had serious hesitation in pursuing my graduate degree because *if I stayed home and worked, I could help my family, and they desperately needed it.* So while people in stable financial situations have their parents funding and providing support for their college situation, many in low socioeconomic situations are in the exact opposite situation, trying to figure out how to navigate college and career on their own while also providing financial support to home. Leaving to start a career might be viewed as selfish. I know many people who opted not to leave home or chose to return home because of this, their aspirations abandoned to help deal with the cycle of poverty and trauma at home.

Often, judgment on the lower classes will counter with the point that, yes, there are these challenges, but in America, given the right steps, there is access to help and support, and one can "pull themselves up by their bootstraps." In certain situations, this is true, but it is often one of those self-serving comments. It is much easier to cherry-pick examples of low-income people who have succeeded than it is to critically consider whether one has had more advantages than another. This second consideration would invite shame, which we desperately try to avoid. It is much easier to demean or lash out at another than to feel personal shame. Put simply, people don't like to think of themselves as having privileges, because they view this as a threat to the idea that they deserve and have earned what they have. Privileges, however, do not speak to whether someone worked hard or not, and they do not mean one's life was without disadvantages or hardship. For example, while there was much in my life holding me back, especially economically, I can't deny that being a straight White male provided me with social advantages and support that helped me climb out of my difficult situation. I didn't just pull myself up on my own. My identity and situation were both disadvantaged and privileged, with the privileges likely being a major part of the reason I was able to translate my hard work into eventual success. By avoiding a shame response and critically examining my personal context, I was able to handle the reality that I had both hardships and advantages and that my success path might not be as easily attainable for others facing the additional barriers of sexism, racism, or transphobia, for example.

Defensiveness and the concept of privilege go hand in hand. An economic example is how people will decry the younger generation, saying that they had nothing handed to them and had to work to pay for their college education. While this is true, in decades past, a college education was affordable, and working could pay for the costs. This is an advantage most do not have in today's world, with the average college debt approaching $30,000 for a bachelor's degree. People like to lead with what disadvantages they had (I didn't have a silver spoon; I had to *work* to get my education) in order to disprove the narrative that they had some type of advantageous situation or support. These things are far from exclusive—all of us have varying levels of advantages and disadvantages based on our context, identity, and life experiences, but seldom do we like to consider the help we've gotten that others cannot access.

We like to paint ourselves as the hero, as if what we've accomplished is solely the product of our own efforts. This is why the bootstraps narrative is kept alive; we like to imagine we simply did what anyone else can do. This allows us to feel talented and special. We don't like to acknowledge that our path may be unobtainable to others due to circumstance, or that in their situation we also may have failed. Sure, you're aware of plenty of supports a poor person could use on their journey up, but you were made aware of those supports, you were taught how to access and use them, and you were given the foundation to stand on to reach for them. Without this awareness, there are powerful voices in the media keeping alive the harmful narrative that poverty is self-inflicted or a moral flaw.

Examples of these differences in viewpoint and access to resources come to mind regarding my work at Penn State as a career counselor. Students from higher-income backgrounds walked into sessions having a sense of what they needed. They were seeking resources for internships, networking, and resume refinement. Students from first-generational, low-income backgrounds often came uncertain as to what questions they even needed to ask. What was career development, and what did they need to do to figure out how to get a job?

Social capital is the sociological concept that refers to the value of social networks and relationships within a society. For our internship example, having a father who is CEO of a major company is high social capital if you're looking to get a job in that company. Having neighbors with professional connections or access to resources is also a form of social capital. Even having a tight-knit community itself allows access to the social networks and ladders that provide advancement. To illustrate this point: Having worked in career services, with access to some of the most up-to-date research on career attainment, I can tell you that the number-one way to guarantee getting a position is not qualifications, skills, ability, or personality—it's by knowing someone in a position of influence.

Networking is a social norm within higher-social-status communities. It is understood as a vehicle of professional advancement and a necessity of career development. I worked with several student clients who informed me that they joined fraternities and sororities on campus solely for the sake of having networking contacts within business fields. These contacts proved fruitful in every case.

As a low-income rural college student, I once viewed networking as vile. How could you use someone else for your own needs? This view is more prevalent in low-income communities, where authenticity and transparency are higher core values than social positioning or professionalism. I also didn't understand what fraternities or sororities really were or why they were appealing. I had absolutely no sense of their social networking function nor that they were disproportionately filled with students of higher social classes who had heard of the norms and advantages of these groups from their college-educated parents.

Further, I didn't know what an internship was or that it was necessary. My parents viewed a college education as all that was needed to get a job, and so did I. I found these realities to be consistent with many first-generation, low-income students I counseled at Penn State. Many were overwhelmed by networking and internships and had never before made a professional resume. They didn't have access to these forms of human capital and did not have parents telling them what steps to take next.

Those born into higher socioeconomic contexts are less likely to be aware of their advantages, because for them these are simply "normal." They are everyday functions and the same treatment others in their community receive. Those born outside these contexts are more likely to notice the privilege that comes with these associations. Being aware of one's own socioeconomic context, privileges, and disadvantages is key in understanding what frameworks have developed our opinions of self, others, and appropriate behavior.

Our socioeconomic context provides the framework by which we judge how to appropriately live and spend money in society. For example, my socioeconomic framework taught me to always seek the "deals" in stores. Quality of items purchased was less important than the price of the item itself. Dollar stores were a premium location to get good deals and spend as little money as possible. This was so that money was conserved and could go as far as possible. Perhaps paradoxically, I also learned that while you want money to go as far as possible, you are supposed to *spend money while you have it*.

This is a perspective those not raised in poverty often judge and critique. I was legitimately surprised as an adult when I learned that many people of a higher socioeconomic status proportionally do not spend a great deal of their money. I was under the assumption that they threw money around without regard for cost of anything. When I got to know people of a higher socioeconomic status, I was astounded by just how integrated into their mindset saving and conserving money was. Saving and investing were completely foreign concepts to me given how I was raised.

This mindset often invites societal critiques. Some may say that those in poverty should save, invest, and be more responsible with their money. While this can be true in some cases, it is also imposing one's context upon another and ignoring the reality of their struggles. I had learned to spend money while you have it for several valid reasons: People of lower socioeconomic status often live in conditions that promote lower quality of health and living standards, resulting in shorter life spans. Indeed, many people in my extended family died early in life, affecting my view on the world. My mother had a phrase growing up that was something akin to "You save, save, and save, and then you die." This hit on the perspective that some in poverty have: Life is short, and tragedy can happen at any time, so spend the money and enjoy the moments while you can.

And when I say tragedy, I don't only mean death. With little in the bank, the car breaking down means a complete disaster. Any misstep leads to a serious financial crisis, which unfortunately becomes the normal state for many families. After all, a 2017 survey from Bankrate indicated that 57% of American families could not afford an emergency expense of $500 or more. Thus, with the constant threat of your money disappearing, there is a pressure to go out and eat while you can or splurge suddenly on a new video game. People in poverty are often under the crushing weight of anxiety, and the ability to spend money is a temporary escape most in their situation would gladly take—that moment of power in a largely powerless situation.

Let's consider an example of this with homeless populations. I've heard people denounce some homeless individuals who were spending what little money they had on alcohol. This, they believed, was an awful use of the money they begged for and assured their continued situation. While alcohol certainly wasn't helpful for these homeless individuals' improving their situation, the judgmental tones I heard raised questions in my mind.

What do people in America often do to "take the edge off" a hard day? They have a drink or two, they go to the bar—it's an accepted social convention. Alcohol and drugs are a temporary escape from the anxieties and pressures of life. The people judging these homeless people were those who often indulged in that very behavior—they loved a drink after a tough day, yet they were so critical of the homeless individuals for spending their money on alcohol. I wondered, given the intense difficulties of homeless life, if these judgmental individuals would grind it out, saving up every single penny and enduring countless hardships and setbacks to slowly rise up, or if they'd spend the few dollars they had on a distraction to make the difficulties just a little bit easier for a moment. Although the judgmental people would probably disagree, I'd venture to say that if they were in the homeless individuals' situation, they, too, would be spending money on alcohol.

The more one accepts and loves themselves, and I mean true love, not egotism or narcissism, generally the more understanding and empathetic they are toward others and their situations. This makes me wonder if harsh judgment is simply a symptom of projection—if they drank in that situation, they would feel shame and weakness, and they are unable to believe they might actually be that exact person if the conditions were right. They blame "the other" to avoid self-judgment.

This is important to consider when we think of "advice" to give others regarding their lifestyle and financial habits. What background are we coming from with our thoughts and perspectives? What background is the other individual coming from? Do I even know these facts and details? Why do I have these automatic thoughts about the situation, whether they are positive or negative?

I say this because much of the advice those in a higher socioeconomic status give to those in a lower socioeconomic status comes off as tone-deaf and unhelpful. It comes without a contextual understanding of the lived reality of people in these situations. Investing, saving, and college planning are much different realities and require much different methods for people barely keeping their heads above water.

Likewise, individuals in low socioeconomic situations often have skewed views of the reality of those in a higher socioeconomic status, assuming in them more negative traits and biases than what exist. Certainly, many people of a higher socioeconomic status are unaware of the reality of individuals in poverty and may give insensitive advice, but often this comes from a true ignorance—not having exposure to or understanding of individuals who were raised in this context. Having individuals in this community seek understanding is key—traveling to these communities, talking with these people, getting involved with charity (the nuts and bolts, instead of only giving money) provide further insight and dialogue, which can increase the understanding, perspective, and empathy of all involved.

I've certainly seen it in my own life, though certainly my examples aren't overarching. In meeting people from communities of a high socio-economic status, I was shocked to see how *nice* and *kind* they were. I had this conception that all of them would be driven by greed and would judge me harshly because of my background. These conceptions were based on media portrayals, both news stories and movies, since my exposure to people with higher wealth than myself was limited. I found that many of these people were kind but were isolated in their own contextual bubbles, truly having no sense of the reality of poor living and having their own biases from media portrayals.

While this is a true example, there is a contextual red flag that must be raised. My mostly positive experience in high-income communities comes with the caveat that I am a White male, and these communities were almost entirely White in composition. I looked the part, so to speak, and my White-ness likely contributed to how easily my cultural background and worldviews were accepted. This segues well into our next topic, how cultural identity and context come into play with how we view and interact with the entire world around us.

chapter seven

Culture and Context

L et's engage in an exercise I often use with my graduate students training to be professional counselors. I'd like you to make a list on a sheet of paper. Please list the top five types of identifiers of a person you would be most comfortable meeting and speaking with. This shouldn't be a person you already know—instead imagine you are going to have a long conversation with a random person. When I ask for a list of the top five identifiers, I mean things like their racial, religious, sexual, class, or gender identity, along with things such as job or hobby roles. If you sat down across from this type of person and had to share details about yourself and your life, who would be least intimidating to do this with?

Please write out five identifiers, and be honest—this is for you, not for me. Analyze the identifiers you came up with. Are there any commonalities between them? Do you have a certain type of person in mind? Why might you list these specific characteristics? Life experience? Familiarity with this type of person? Similarity to yourself? It makes sense that many of us would likely list a person with at least a few of the same cultural characteristics of ourselves. That would make talking about one's self and feeling understood easier, right?

A major influence on how we view self and the world is through the social construction of our identity. Our families, environments, communities, and life situations all contribute to how we are aware of identity, relation to others, and preferred roles in society. Who we are raised around, identify with, feel close to, and build community with influences how we view the world, connect with others, and build the structure of self.

If I ask you to imagine a medical doctor, what image comes to mind? What are the top five identifiers of that person? What is their race, gender, sexual orientation, and class of origin? If I ask you to imagine a criminal, what is their race, gender, sexual orientation, and class of origin? If I ask you to imagine a teacher, a nurse, a politician—what do you come up with? If I say the word *safe*, what type of person comes to mind? What about *dangerous*?

How did you come up with these identifiers? Were all of them grounded in your experience of the world? Were some of them influenced by media portrayals? Were those portrayals accurate? Did they have bias? Were some of these questions comfortable or uncomfortable?

The high school I went to was about 95% White during my tenure there. One day, while walking through the halls, I saw someone who would one day become a friend of mine. He was a Black male, tall and well built, his hair styled in long dreadlocks. I'd never seen him before, and here was my initial mental reaction:

"Uh-oh, there's trouble."

This was one of the first times in my life that I challenged my own thoughts. I wondered why I had been worried at the sight of another kid just walking down the hall. I stopped and asked myself: *Where did that reaction come from?*

This is something that we rarely do. Our minds treat our innate thoughts and reactions as correct and necessary to navigate the world. Thus, rather than feeling shame over our thoughts, we put up barriers and justify them with any "facts" we can. In this situation, I realized that I essentially had had no prolonged experience in my entire life with people of color. All I had known was media portrayals. This lack of experience and skewed media portrayals of people of color had fostered a racist reaction within me. I recognized that this was inaccurate and harmful, especially as I got to know this friend. I am grateful for the conversations and guidance he gave me in my life journey.

I'd like you to list the top five identifiers of a person you would be LEAST comfortable meeting and talking with for the first time. Please include cultural identifiers such as race, gender, sexual orientation, class status, religious beliefs, or whatever others are salient for you. If you had to meet this person and talk deeply about yourself, you would be quite uncomfortable.

Is the type of person you came up with similar to you in many ways? I'm going to venture a guess that they are quite different. I imagine that you either had a negative experience with this type of person or you have limited experience with this type of person and thus experience anxiety. We are wired to be scared of what is new and different, and this often has us othering people.

I was part of this process when I saw my future friend in the hall. My mind had othered him due to his cultural characteristics. I could be defensive about this reaction, buying into the worry and refusing to challenge myself in order to avoid shame, but this would burrow me in ignorance and prevent growth. If I was to learn and grow as a person, moving toward more positivity and connectedness, I had to be willing to face what I felt and where it had come from.

Stereotypical and racist media portrayals are everywhere. They are historically integrated into our culture and have permeated outward to the degree that people believe them to be hard fact. That is how our minds are designed: to defend our innate stances and protect our own identity. To avoid shame, people often justify their feelings. They claim that it isn't about race, it's just about style and dress, and that if people don't want to be viewed a certain way, they shouldn't dress and represent themselves in a certain way. This is forcing a cultural norm on another set of people, as well as victim-blaming. It is essentially saying, "Don't inconvenience me with your reality; instead conform to my own. I don't want to think that I am bad or think bad things, therefore I am leaning on this other interpretation that you should conform to."

It's much easier to live in a world where people are responsible for and have control of how they are received, what they achieve, and what doors open for them. For many White people, there was a degree of that control in their lives. It's tough to think that this may come at the expense of others who were not afforded the same opportunities. Thus, instead of feeling bad (White guilt) about this, many justify their stances, denying things like racism and privilege with "facts" and "examples" they bring up, claiming others are "making it about race."

Bias against other races, genders, sexual orientations, ability statuses, or other classes isn't a zero-sum game. Often, unproductive conversations happen when one suggests they cannot be racist or sexist or transphobic because they have a friend within that category or have expressed kind sentiments in the past. This is a tactic used to avoid the shame that comes with potentially realizing one has done something wrong. If a "fact" can justify and explain a behavior, one does not have to face its root and instead is able to live comfortably (at least temporarily) in their constructed reality.

Bias occurs on a spectrum. We all have biases toward and against certain groups of people based on race, gender, culture, religion, socio-economic status, ability status, you name it, all based on our world contexts and experiences. We all have automatic reactions that are problematic. The issue becomes this: Many of us want to avoid that reality in order to feel like we're a good person. Instead of listening when someone calls out something we've done, we instead treat them like a threat and put our walls up. The growth and connection opportunity is thus thwarted, because we wish to avoid shame and have treated this instance like a zero-sum game.

Be aware of any defensive reactions you have. Defensiveness serves to protect your own reality and keep you burrowed in the cave from Plato's allegory we mentioned earlier in the book. Defensiveness is meant to allow you to survive but not thrive. In social settings, this defensiveness from shame doesn't truly help us in the long run, and instead buries us in our own biases and shortcomings. By checking in with yourself when you are feeling defensive, you can evaluate whether you should drop the defenses, be more open, and listen.

Within counseling, there is a professional obligation to work toward multicultural competence. I always let my graduate students know that multicultural competence is not something they simply attain. It is something continually worked toward, with a counselor encouraged to explore their biases, work through them, work on learning about other populations, open the conversation about potential bias or disconnect in session, and realize that they will always be growing in this domain. The world is always changing, and thus we are always gaining new insight into the lived experiences of others. Our competence is forever a work in progress. Similarly, in everyday life, we are constantly encountering new people and situations. If we are mindful about our reactions and open to understanding the lived reality of another, we are inviting growth and connection into our world.

Studies show that counselors are more effective with clients of different cultural backgrounds than themselves when they introduce the topic of identity into the conversation. Clients from marginalized backgrounds may feel uncertain whether they can bring this aspect of their identities into the room or if the counselor will be unaware or dismissive. When a counselor opens this door, they show a willingness to truly listen, hear, respect, and value the client. Rather than avoidance of the topic, this is a recognition that cultural differences are real and are a real part of the client's experience.

As a counselor, I've worked on always bringing my identity into the room when working with clients from different backgrounds. I let them know that as a White male, I may be unaware of certain aspects of their experience or may even appear insensitive or dismissive of something due to my lack of understanding. I let the client or supervisee know that this is not my intention and I wish to learn and grow in this process as well, and I invite them to bring any issues with these things into the room as they occur. This has resulted in several very deep and fruitful conversations with clients who felt weights lifted off their shoulders because I was acknowledging the reality of the experience. One client in particular informed me that this moment was when she knew she could actually trust me, because I was willing to address the actual dynamics in the room. She was happy that I wasn't defensive about my identity and was willing to be corrected by her if I had a faulty interpretation. This allowed us to develop a healthy rapport, which was crucial in her getting the most she could out of the counseling experience.

As a male counselor who worked with female children who had experienced sexual abuse at the hands of male perpetrators, if I ignored my identity in the counseling room, I would be doing a great disservice, and perhaps even emotional harm, to my clients. I had to be aware of my tone of voice, my positioning in the room, the suddenness of my motions, and the process of transference within the room. It would be natural for some of these children to be afraid of me or dislike me because of my identity. If I became at all defensive toward these reactions and dismissive of the validity of them, I could be retraumatizing children who, understandably, had difficulty connecting with older adult males. I found that being aware of who I was and how I presented, and being open to all reactions, allowed me to establish therapeutic relationships with these children, assisting in their ability to trust, grow, and flourish.

It can be difficult realizing that our view of the world is shaped by our cultural standing and that perhaps parts of our identity have been favored. As part of my graduate training, I engaged in several privilege walks. This is when the class steps forward for every statement that aligns with their life experience in a positive way (getting some type of advantage) and takes a step backward for every life experience that was a barrier (experiencing oppression based on identity). Despite my class status, I was always near or at the front by the end of these experiences. My classmates of marginalized identities were always farther back due to experiencing overt oppression and heightened anxiety due to how they were perceived in society. I could have retreated into my shell to avoid feeling shame, or I could have lashed out and challenged the validity of their experiences, but these reactions would have been harmful to me and them. Instead, it was critical that I open my mind and heart to understand their context and lived experience. Through their context, I could further understand how the world operated not just for me, but for many others, and develop a deep sense of meaning from this.

I've had several conversations with individuals from different backgrounds than myself regarding the experience of my hometown. While I was often supported and heard in my community, providing me a sense of connection and an idea of what the community was, several friends of mine had markedly different experiences based on the color of their skin, their religion, their sexual orientation, and their gender. School had not been as warm or welcoming, groups of people had taunted and bullied, strangers in the community had made threats—all things that had never happened to me and I had been unaware of.

What is the reality of my home community? Is it the place that treated me one way? Does my experience give my community definition and erase the validity of the experiences of others? It's important to realize that our experience and context is our own, and those with different identities often have markedly different experiences. If we aren't considering the truth of others, we are straying from the truth of ourselves and the environments we operate within. We love the world to be simply black and white, right and wrong, but often the environments we interact with are mired in those shades of gray in between.

Think about your own racial and cultural reality. What makes you comfortable? What makes you feel at home? What type of people remind you of home? What type of celebrations make you feel happy? What type of food makes you feel like yourself? We all have cultural identity integrated at the core of who we are. It's natural that we prefer things that make us feel safe and comfortable—secure in what the world "should" be, an image formed back when we were a child. Unfortunately, we don't always go beyond those "shoulds" and consider how we're looking at the world and why. We're not always giving ourselves a chance to learn, grow, connect, and self-actualize.

Identity models highlight this well. Most models highlight how those of minority status have an awareness of their race much earlier in life due to activating events. They are made to feel different and often don't see people like them portrayed positively or frequently in media. They are aware of society's label on them as "the other." White identity models highlight how Whites are unaware and unquestioning of their identity due to a lack of these events. When these events occur, Whites often avoid or justify actions to avoid shame, and then eventually feel great guilt or hopelessness when they realize their own racist views and actions. This can be paralyzing for Whites, who avoid the conversation due to this shame and may not work toward growth. Eventually, Whites can become more aware of their views, challenging themselves and other Whites when they arise, and eventually commit themselves to directly antiracist action to help shift the tide of society.

Many Whites experiencing guilt will highlight the nice things they've done for people of color or loudly share their progressive views regarding race. This is often an attempt to be free of the burden of their own shame and guilt. The truth is, however, it is not a zero-sum game. Racism and bias are truly a spectrum, and we should all always be working through our thoughts and feelings. As a counselor, I'm still actively challenging myself, listening, inviting new conversations, and exploring my biases and anxieties. I'm willing to be wrong about things. I'm willing to listen. I know that this willingness to learn and grow is more important than saving face and avoiding uncomfortable emotions. If I'm going to connect with and help people, I have to be willing to be corrected and truly hear them out.

Listening is key. I recall a time during my master's program when a classmate, Tony, was concerned about how the class responded to a professor. As a class, we'd made plans for getting this professor a present because he'd brought food to class on several occasions and treated us kindly. Tony, who was Black, brought up the fact that although other professors, including those of color, had done kind things for us, we hadn't tried to get them something. He said he felt that since this professor was a White male, we might feel more inclined to reward him over these other professors, and he worried about the signal this would send.

Several individuals in the classroom were hesitant to listen to Tony's viewpoint. The possibility that our perceptions were altered due to identity were uncomfortable. I spoke up in support of Tony and thought we truly had to consider this possibility if we were to understand what was going on. Tony and I spoke after class. He was appreciative that I was willing to talk through these things, and we had a deep conversation about race and identity within education. This set a norm between us in which we were "willing to go there," which helped us be more honest with one another and which allowed for joint learning. Thanks to those conversations, we ended up using our joint experiences and perspective to give a professional presentation on race and identity, allowing others to consider these issues and their own teaching styles. If I had chosen to give credit to an initial reaction of defensiveness, I would have alienated myself from a growth opportunity and the development of a wonderful friendship.

We yearn to be validated. We want to hear we are right. We want to get what we want. Media and politicians know this very well. Our tendencies to defend our own experience and views becomes weaponized against us. The media now serves a role in keeping us aware of all the "foul" things groups of "the other" are doing. Our anxiety is piqued, we believe those others are wretched, and we burrow into our biases, far away from growth and connection. Politicians speak this language, trying to get us to associate with them and support them despite their hypocrisy, flaws, and special interests. This language is everywhere, but we cannot begin to challenge these structures if we are not first challenging ourselves. If we feed our egos and biases, they grow within us and become more defensive, more unwilling to allow us to change through education and connection.

The media continues making money from likes, shares, and outrage, and politicians keep getting elected despite their lack of performance or a true platform. If we begin listening and seeing each other as people, then we begin the process of working through our own biases. This allows us to avoid exploitation and division, empowering us to come together for the betterment of society.

Be willing to critically engage in how culture and experience have constructed your worldview. How do you relate to your culture? How does your culture relate to society? What experiences have made you aware of parts of your identity? What can you do to better understand the identity and lived experiences of others? When do you become defensive and why? How has that defensiveness caused stress or limitations in your life? By being open and thoughtful rather than anxious and defensive, you can live a warmer, healthier life, rife with meaningful connection.

chapter eight

Generational Context

F rom birth to age 5, we go from being incapable in almost every single way to being able to walk, run, jump, speak a language fluently, and understand social and academic concepts. Never again in our lives will we develop at such a rapid rate, our mind and body growing to understand ourselves and the world. It makes sense, then, that so many of us develop our sense of identity and relation to the world in these pivotal years. It also makes sense that, for those of us who have experienced trauma during this time, life can be completely flipped upside down from the timing of these major disruptions. The lens we develop in our childhood encompasses our first (and most solid) conceptions of the world—how we believe it is and how we believe it *should* be.

It's common to hear people reflect fondly on the good ol' days, or a period in their lives that they romanticize. They will claim life was simpler, the world was safer, and entertainment was better. They yearn for the simplicity of this supposed gilded age, and why wouldn't they? Something to note when evaluating these comments is the era in question. Very commonly, people will select a time when they were kids or teenagers as being the best. This has much to do with context. This was the time when we figured out how the world is supposed to work. This was when we had our first exposure to entertainment. This was when our brain made neural connections around understanding what things were and why. The rest of our lives were filtered through these initial experiences.

These things occur in our childhood and are essential in developing our context and identities. We learn who we are in relation to others, how people are supposed to act, what the world is like, and what quality entertainment is. This is the structure and understanding we crave from the world and the sort that allows us to function well. A key point to consider in this is our access to information. As children, we are greatly unaware of the ills of the world: the great tragedies and daily violence, how unfair systems truly are, and how the good guy doesn't always win in the end. The world seems safer because the world is smaller, and we haven't yet had to deal with messy complications.

Our access to information today is greater than it has ever been. If a murder occurs on the other side of the planet, we have the ability to learn about it in mere minutes. Every tragedy, murder, injustice—we are bombarded with images and information from social media, news websites, and entertainment. And these things sell; news media portrays all of the dangerous aspects of the world, with killings and crimes the top stories, delivered right to us.

It is understandable, then, that one would yearn for the experience of the world they had in their childhood. The world made more sense due to their limited information, their ignorance acting as a buffer. The entertainment they liked and understood was what was popular and accessible. They knew how the world worked because society hadn't yet shifted and changed, and they didn't need to be bothered with questions of whether society was truly just and fair for all. We tend to treat the world as if it exists for us—we are upset when society changes. We feel left behind and confused as the world takes a new course. But the world has always been doing this—we just associate the reality of the world with the period in which we learned our own norms. And given how we so easily see the flaws in others while justifying or ignoring those in ourselves, it is easy to understand why a person from one generation decries the lifestyle and values of a younger generation, despite the fact that there is always plenty to critique about the past. In a way, childhood is the cave we were raised in, again borrowing from Plato's allegory. As we grow older, we are exposed to more truths of the world, which are troubling and which we often wish to reject.

The complicated realities of history and society are difficult to swallow. For example, the violent crime rate has steadily dropped over the years. Students of history will know how violent and dangerous this world has been throughout time, including within the last 100 years. Murder and illness (particularly the infant death rate) were rampant compared to what they are today. People tend not to believe this due to how inundated we are with media sharing with us every ill that occurs in the world. Similar ills and even worse ones have always occurred—we just weren't always made aware of them.

We tend to ignore how the past had more crime, more injustice, less access to services and education, and how, comparatively, the world is more equal than it has ever been. This statement actually is likely to be controversial to others who are ready to point out all the negative aspects of the world. Yes, these things are a reality, but the overarching reality is that they have always been horrible in many facets throughout human history, and we are simply learning more about them and making small bits of progress on them as time continues.

From an existential perspective, it is difficult living in a world that doesn't make sense to us. When we experience how gray morality and structure can be in society, when we are faced with the troubling truths of systemic racism and historical injustice, when we're forced to question people and entertainment we've held dear, our identities are threatened. The building blocks from which we've constructed ourselves are being pulled away and our defense mechanisms tell us that we are going to collapse. Therefore, we wall up, deny it, and blame others and the world for what's going on. The world needs to be one thing, the thing we believe, and other people are preventing that from happening, and thus we are bitter toward them. This is self-serving in the immediate protective sense, but in the long-term, it isolates us from the truth and from other people.

Cognitive behavioral therapy focuses on "shoulds" and "musts"— these tell us what cognitive self-talk is harmful to a client. If we believe the world "should" or "must" be something, when truly it isn't beholden to our single view, we are likely to be frustrated and disappointed. We are likely to be filled with anxiety and feelings of hopelessness. The things we designate as necessary aren't panning out, and we feel powerless to help and full of bitterness toward others. If we don't catch ourselves in the "musts" and "should," we're destined to be disappointed by a world that will not conform to us. This isn't to say we shouldn't alter or change the world for the better through political and social movements, but rather that if we try to make the world something based on our sole view of what is right and proper from our childhood, then we are destined to feel negative feelings when it doesn't play out.

When we reflect on a golden era in our past, we are negating the experience of others. Namely, those for whom the era was not ideal. For those who glorify the 1950s, for example, it was a time of even more severe racial inequity. Those who glorify it glorify their world experience as a child and a valuation of the norms they learned but don't consider the full scope of the era. This is true of any era, including our own, and it is natural to desire the norms we became familiar with early in life, but if we pine for this without critically considering what was good and bad about the time period, we're not fully considering how we were shaped by our context and how that muddies our view of the current world.

If we're caught in a contextual past, it may be difficult to adjust to and work within the present. If we believe the world is the cause of our woes, we deny ourselves the self-responsibility necessary to make changes in our lives. We cannot make a positive difference for ourselves and others if we are focused on a defeatist belief that the world was once better and that forces beyond our control inhibit success. By letting go and realizing that our conceptions of a golden age are a self-creation, we free ourselves to analyze the current world with less bias and take the steps toward making life better for ourselves and others.

When you look at nationalistic movements, you must ask, what desire is at the root of these? It is an attempt to "restore" the world to a desired state based on a previous contextual reality. Namely, the world is moving in a direction that is dismaying to people compared to their early life conceptions. For example, nationalistic movements yearn for a "purer" society of Americans (i.e., White Christians and their values), which is likely fueled by a nostalgic view of this experience in their childhood. These people were raised in a White Christian context with those values. They enjoy them and have fond memories centered around them. They have since learned more about the world and seen the country, as it naturally does, shift in different social directions, with inclusion and diversity increasingly spreading as a value. These people are made anxious and afraid by change, insecure in the idea of a world outside their control, and attempt to seize control of reality by imposing their worldview and standards upon others through hatred and violence.

When the world is difficult for us to understand, we yearn for the simplicity and comfort of childhood. Unfortunately, for many, that results in lashing out at the world and those who are different, as they are the perceived sources of "ruining" the world. Really, this is just the process of separate realities coming into contact. America has always been multinational and multiethnic. After hundreds of years of struggles for equality, of sharing the lived reality of their struggle, women and minorities are having their stories told more often and are influencing the direction of society in a larger way than in the past. It is not that these people and their realities are new; it's that their voices are being heard more frequently. This conflicts with the reality held sacred by those with nationalistic principles, and rather than become introspective upon this, it is easier to blame "the other" as wrong and corrupted.

If we're living unaware of how context shapes us and what we claim to believe to be the right path for the world, we're likely to find ourselves spiraling down a path of violence and tragedy. A gilded view of an age shaped by the norms of the dominant group paves way for intellectual justification of oppression of others. How do we move forward in a world where people have such clearly different viewpoints on what happened during world events and what it all means? How do we manage our stress and anxieties in such a plugged-in and conflict-laden world? The final chapter ahead tries to take the content of this book and instill it into some mindful approaches to surviving the world in these multiple realities.

chapter nine

Living Mindfully in Context

H ave you ever met someone who is very flippant with their identity and lifestyle? By this I mean someone who follows trends, fads, or movements, so much so that they appear to be a completely different person every few years? It can be someone who drastically changes with each romantic relationship, involves themselves with cult-like groups and movements, or has darted all around the political spectrum. What is going on with one of these people? Why are they seemingly so different in what they follow and believe in with every shift in their life?

If we don't do the work to build the foundation of ourselves, we rely on external sources for our identity. If we don't look deep within ourselves, a scary process that many avoid, we end up chasing groups, movements, and ideas that can give us identity. If we harken back to existential principles, we're so afraid of innately being nothing that we don't think about it and instead believe in whatever we are involved with currently. Others accept us, acknowledge us, love us, and thus we have found meaning—or so we think.

Existentialism leans on the premise that existence is innately meaninglessness and it is our responsibility to face it and then create our own meaning. Otherwise, we slap labels on ourselves and live moment to moment, with principle and philosophy secondary to our avoidance of introspection. It is a difficult thing for many people to consider who they are or what their purpose is if you take away their affiliations. Think about it ... you ask certain people to imagine what life would be like if we found out there was no God, or if we found out their political candidate had always been lying, or that their loved one isn't right for them ... and what do you get? People say this can't be imagined, it's pointless to do so; they lash out at the question, or they demean the perceived "other."

I personally think one's spiritual beliefs are deeper and more personally intimate when they have been challenged. If one has considered and even accepted the possibility that there is no God or meaning, yet still concludes that they believe in God and innate meaning, I think that is a true, meaningful belief at the core of a person's being. If a person does not go through this process of consideration, they may be blinded by their fears and biases, to the degree where they don't actually understand who they are and therefore believe in and join movements to avoid wrestling with difficult concepts.

It is generally easier in life for us to identify what we are not, or what we currently are not. Rather than find out what we are and build a self, it is much easier to knock down the selves of others. If someone who is a Republican is challenged about Donald Trump, often their response is to knock Obama, Biden, or Hillary Clinton. The central question about Trump isn't addressed or introspected upon—it is dismissed as an attack by "the other," and the perceived wrongness of "the other" is used to justify avoidance of contemplation.

It makes sense why people operate like this. Shame is powerful, and facing the fact that we may be wrong is something we avoid from childhood. What if everything we believe is wrong? What if we have been misled? What if we really don't know too much of anything?

Existential therapy rebrands this as liberating. Meaninglessness is not floating adrift on a vast sea of nothingness—it is you having the power to chart your course and set sail in whichever direction you choose. Now, this isn't nihilism—it isn't just about following whatever impulse you want—usually the most fulfilling lives are those linked to principle, causes, and meaningful activity such as charity.

Think of how far we will go to avoid facing who we are. I'm sure you've seen plenty of people obsess about their romantic relationships. In this situation, there are plenty of times when the person in the relationship is secondary to the fact that the person has a relationship at all. We've likely all seen situations where people continue to date those who aren't good for them, only to jump into a similar relationship (often with a very different person) after the conclusion of the former relationship. Often, we want to be defined by our romantic relationships.

We want someone to love us, to make us worthy, and to project the idea of happily ever after. Think about it—you are unique, special, and wonderful. You are *everything* to someone. You exist as part of a perfect relationship, which will mean a happy marriage and life.

We have these ideals, and it makes sense. We don't have to work on ourselves, we don't have to grow, we don't have to face our flaws or uncertainties. Another person takes those away. This person makes us who we are supposed to be—someone who is loved, coveted, and complete. The reason people chase this ideal is because, in the short run, it works and is appealing, but in the long run, it doesn't work out. Like an addict, we pursue temporary flashes of completion instead of doing the work to truly achieve it over time.

The existential principle of isolation touches on this. It claims that we can never be anyone else but who we are. We cannot be defined or exist within a relationship—we are isolated from the thoughts and reality of the other person. We can still have wonderful and loving relationships ... but we are two separate people who are actively choosing to work to make this relationship last. The other person does not define us, take away our responsibility, or solve our woes. They may help us in these endeavors, but the relationship itself doesn't do it for us. We have to continually make active choices and keep working on building ourselves. This isn't the fairy-tale romance. This isn't someone seeing us and realizing we are perfect and devoting themselves to us every moment for the rest of our life. This is introspection and daily work, which helps us grow stronger, wiser, and more complete.

There was someone I went to high school with who idealized the concept of her wedding and happily ever after. She pushed for marriage in every relationship she got into, regardless of the man she was dating. It didn't seem to be about the person she was with; rather, these men were simply possibilities that made her fantasy possible. Her perfect reality, a wedding symbolizing she was worthy of love and happily ever after, needed a participant. Thus, who a person was became secondary to the role they could play for her. These relationships failed, and this person continually questioned why she had such bad luck with love and why she didn't deserve a happily ever after. When my friend defended these men (who often treated her badly) or her relationship decisions, she wasn't truly defending these things; what she was doing was saying, "Stop trying to take my happily ever after away from me."

This reminds me of how many clients feel when they come into counseling. They seek the love of a significant other or family member who is mistreating them. If only they can earn this person's love or change them, they can prove that they are worth loving. They have it stuck in their mind that this other person's approval is necessary for self-love. They chase the feelings they never give themselves, fleeting moments of love, fleeting sensations of completion, yet they do this at the expense of their long-term happiness. They chase something they've created, putting stock in an external figure who they hope can grant them completion. True self-understanding and love come from within, from deep contemplation and acceptance.

Chasing the ideal to avoid meaninglessness prevents us from doing the work to clearly realize who we are, what we believe in, where we need to grow, and how to get to where we want to be. We are sold these distractions on a daily basis. Reality television shows, many of them focusing on love, smartphones, video games, beauty products, clothing—these help us *become* someone or *escape* reality. There's nothing wrong with these products in moderation, but they are often sold to us as a means for us to avoid really dealing with the difficult questions and thoughts lurking in our minds. If we don't deal with those and figure out who we are, we will always be chasing something, never quite know what that is, and blame the world when we don't get it.

Let's bring this example back to childhood. As children, if we were offered unlimited sweet treats, such as ice cream and cookies, many of us would indulge. We would eat poorly and ask for more, more, more. If our caregivers allowed it, we would become gluttons, eating away carefree and likely developing health problems. We'd lack energy and health and have poor emotional responses as well. But why? We got what we wanted! We desired the treats and received a temporary boost of happiness when we consumed them. Why in the world would we become sickly and miserable?

In many ways, we never grow up. We still are those children. Our sweets may be relationships, sex, gambling, television, video games, social media, our job, our image, or many other things. We want a temporary burst of happiness, a glimpse of completion, validation, and recognition that makes us feel worthy, but oftentimes we consume at the expense of our long-term completion. We chase and chase and chase fleeting moments and impulses, all to avoid doing the hard work that can allow us to create our meaning, purpose, and happy lives.

As children, we have parents who impose rules and restrictions. This prevents us, in most cases, from simply indulging in whatever

we'd like. As adults, however, we don't quite have the same bound-
aries. We become convinced that we know what is best for ourselves
and are in control of our habits, and we treat others who challenge us
as purely antagonistic. Why do they have to get on our backs? Why
don't they understand what this habit does for us? Why can't they get
our justification? When sources (inward or outward) challenge these
pursuits, we become defensive. We either don't want to face reality
(leave our caves), or we desperately wish to avoid any self-judgment
or shame. Thus, we continue to avoid growth opportunities, settle for
distractions, and fall further away from our own actualization and
connectedness with others.

Buddhist philosophy has meaningful thoughts on this. When we
focus on the self, we destroy the self. The more we obsess about earning
materials, recognition, and what we deserve, the more we stray from
peace, happiness, and completion. The more we try to impose who
we are or how we are perceived, the more pain and suffering we bring
ourselves, because true completion isn't possible. We will never be
"whole" or "defined" or "successful." We're always a work in progress,
the self is not innate and fluctuates depending on context, and we're
always going to deal with pain and strife. The key is accepting these
things, letting go of our urges and impulses, and living peacefully. We
can accept our own limitations, realize the external world will never
fully fulfill us, and stop act as dogs chasing cars.

Taoism introduced the idea that nothingness, or emptiness, is actually
the natural goal of life, and not something to be avoided. Consider cups
and houses. If these structures were completely filled, they wouldn't be
able to take things inside; they would be unable to fill their purpose. In
the case of a cup, it is the emptiness within which allows it to be filled
with water. In a house, it is the empty space inside which allows it to
become a home. Similarly, in life we are so hyper focused on doing
and becoming that we fill our emptiness and thus lose out. Rather, if
we allow ourselves to be rather than do, the emptiness in us all can be
fulfilled. The nothingness is not a loss, but rather opportunity, and if
we are open and flexible our cups can be filled by the waters of life.
We can be open and present to experience and other people and thus
feel great fulfillment instead of being so concerned with establishing
ourselves, portraying ourselves, asserting ourselves, and ultimately
avoiding ourselves. Our attempts at becoming and finding completion
in the external world actually move us away from allowing ourselves
to be present and fulfilled by our true lived experience.

This is all easier said than done, of course. Not everyone can let go of desires, avoid distractions, and pursue self-actualization. However, this doesn't mean we cannot be critical of our habits. What are we chasing? Why? What does this do for us? Is it healthy? How much have we explored who we are and where our motivations come from? What people in our lives are healthy for us? Which are just distractions? How do we let go of "shoulds" "musts" and preconceptions so that we can presently be in touch with who we are and truly listen to others? How do we get in touch with ourselves in present moments rather than being preoccupied with how we project ourselves to others?

Aristotle introduced the concept of friendships of utility versus friendships of the good. In friendships of utility, people are being used for some purpose. Think of a group of pals who get together to play basketball. They may have their group of good-time friends who come together for competition and distraction, but they may talk about little else, confide in each other rarely if ever, and never do much else together. This friendship serves a purpose as a distraction—each member is using the other friends so that they can play a game.

A friendship of the good exists regardless of activities and free of ulterior motive. A friendship of the good is cemented in an authentic appreciation for who the other person is in a holistic sense. The friend is looked at as a role model, an inspiration, and simply being around them in any capacity feels good. It is never about the activity or roles they are playing—it is simply about who the person is.

Consider the relationships of utility in your life. Who are you using and for what purposes? Who is using you and for what purpose? And this doesn't mean that relationships of utility are always bad. It can be great to have a group of friends in an adult sports league—what a release! However, be wary of confusing relationships of utility with relationships of the good. Often, we don't analyze or evaluate the relationships in our lives or the roles they are playing. Are we surrounding ourselves with people who hold us in mutual regard? Are we around the people who inspire us and are inspired by us? Do the people we associate with truly care about us, and will they be there in good times and bad?

Are we engaging in socialization which promotes authenticity and personal growth? Do we catch ourselves trying to appear a certain way or get certain attention for the sake of avoiding our own feelings of inadequacy? Are we holistically tuning into who we are, what we need, who is healthy to surround ourselves with, and how to communicate these things to ourselves and others? So often in life we react based on the moment, our initial surge of thoughts, feelings, pressures, and anxieties, but these motors usually push us into actions and situations which don't give us what we need.

Contemplation is rare in our society. We are inundated with distractions. Smartphones, social media, television, movies, video games, bright screens, careerism—there's always something more to do. We're pulled away from working on ourselves by the distractions, by the "sweets," the desire to be known and defined as something. Moments in the day of contemplation, meditation, and journaling can help ground us in what is going on, what we are truly feeling, and what we really think. The dark place where our thoughts, feelings, and true selves lurk doesn't have to be scary—it can be a sanctuary, a place for us each to tend to our personal gardens. When we tend to ourselves, who we are can grow and flourish. We can be empowered to see who we are and what we'd like to accomplish in our lives.

I find that once people have a foundation, their affiliation with groups, movements, and activities flourishes in a positive way. Think of a person who has challenged their biases, beliefs, and experiences. If they then come to a conclusion that a particular religion and its values are what they agree with, this is likely a secure decision—they are living in line with their principles. If someone is simply born into a religious belief system, never challenges it, never introspects, and views others who challenge it purely as "the other," they have denied themselves the opportunity of understanding what role their religion plays in their life. They have allowed something else to define them rather than defining themselves and letting it add to the definition. They have a rocky foundation and will spend much of their life patching it to keep it standing rather than building a strong foundation and supplementing the structure with the positive values their religious beliefs provide them. It is similar to relationships of utility versus relationships of the good—do we believe because we are using it for definition, or do we believe because we've done the work to examine it and truly believe?

This is nothing new and radical. As Socrates once said, "The unexamined life is not worth living." While I don't exactly agree on the not-worth-living part, his point is well taken. The examined life is much more deep and fruitful, in my opinion.

All of this work can be done by us examining our own biases and context. What situations have led us to believe what we have? What have we avoided? Where do we need to grow? How does our lens put us in line with the experiences of others? What blinders do we still have? But how, then, do we deal with those who are operating in a different context? We're certainly not all mental health counselors or philosophers.

A simple thing we can do is listen. This is an understated point in our society. So often we are encouraged to share our opinion, to throw it out there on social media, and defend our right to do so. Certainly, we have a right to do this, but we often don't consider whether it is a good thing. The same can be said of in-person interactions. So often we are waiting for our turn to speak, to impose our beliefs, our truth, and our context. So rarely do we listen with fidelity, allowing ourselves to understand the reality of another, especially those who are different from us. Listening with the full mind and heart allows us to find the humanity in others, bridge a connection, and work on joint growth together. When we impose our own context, we are focusing on the self—we are focusing on how we are *different* or *better* than another. When we listen deeply, when we sit with someone and empathize, we focus on the similarities, how we are the *same*, humans deep down, even if there are stark differences. Listening is not only about being present for others but also offers incredible growth for our individual selves. By listening and being present, we turn off our own urges to impose, to be defined, to be known, to be validated, and simply focus on being in the present moment.

It's easy for us to find "definition" and "identity" by separating ourselves from other groups of people. Labels are neat and easy ways for us to be known. However, this is a process of division. We do not truly understand others or recognize their humanity, and thus we destroy potential bridges. Human beings have more commonalities than I could ever state in this book, but we seldom listen to find those connections. We seldom truly want to connect. I encourage all of us to listen more in our lives. To understand, to care, and to connect. And even if there are those we deal with who are rude or vicious, often being pulled into conflict or a cycle of cruel responses doesn't help our well-being. It doesn't help us grow or feel happy. It brings us down, gives us less faith in the world, and leaves us with terrible emotions. As an old Buddhist proverb states, "Holding on to anger is like grasping a hot coal with the intent of throwing it at someone else; you are the one who gets burned."

Gandhi once said, "An eye for an eye makes the whole world blind." Consider this for a moment. So often we are appalled by those who wrong us or others. We develop hatred for them, the same hatred they harbor for us or others. We feel the same vicious feelings, wish harm upon them, and give them no sanctuary in our hearts. Thus, we become like those we hate, happy to inflict pain on others, taking joy in their downfall, and reveling in division. When something bad befalls someone who is cruel in some way, what is our reaction? Often, we are happy because we think the wicked should suffer. We feel as if we've won and they've been put in their place. We feel superior and dance inside. Rarely are our reactions truly about the principles or issues at hand ... do we solemnly celebrate that there is less suffering in the world, or do we loudly boast about how they got what they deserved? These motivations and feelings are quite different, the second fueled by division and a desire to feel superior and have a grasp on law, morality, and justice. I'm not suggesting for us to be ashamed of our human reactions, but rather to analyze them, where they are coming from, and what they do to our emotional state and connectedness to others. How can we find ourselves and inner serenity if we live in a constant cycle of conflict and turbulence? As a counselor, I've gone into most of my sessions with the perspective that most people are suffering in some way. They've been through trials, challenges, pain, division, self-doubt, and so much more. Regardless of whether they are like me or if I even personally like them, I try to listen and understand. I try to see their humanity and empathize, even if they've done terrible things. I try to see how I would be similar if I was in their context, and what this means for how I can help them learn, grow, and become happier and kinder people. My understanding of others is inextricably tied to my understanding of myself. By seeing the similarities and how given the same context I might have ended up similar to other people, I become more in touch with my own humanity. I avoid the whispers of my ego, which demand that I assert myself as different, more enlightened, wiser or better. These urges pull me away from who I truly am, what I need to work on, and how I can be present and productive in everyday moments. The willingness to see and hear others is the willingness to see and hear yourself. It is in recognition of similarities, not differences, that we learn and grow, and once we are willing to see what is truly there we are empowered to sculpt ourselves into the people we aspire to be. I believe that applying the principles of empathy and connectedness to our interactions and conversations in general will be fruitful for all of us. We will unite with more people, developing a shared understanding and context, or at the very least understand the suffering someone is going through (even if they are rude or cruel) and choose not to communicate or associate with them. Thus, we understand ourselves and humanity a little more, and step by step, we are conquering mountains.

Gandhi also said, "Be the change you wish to see in the world." We are constantly goaded by television and social media to look down on the actions of others. We focus on what others are doing wrong, which makes us *feel* right without actually having to do anything right. We are so caught up in how others live that we don't live disciplined, meaningful lives ourselves. Focusing on others and their negativity pull us away from the work each of us must do to learn, grow, and flourish. Each of us has the power to make the world better for others every single day. Each of us can spread kindness, understanding, compassion, and togetherness. This is no small responsibility, and the impact is incredibly huge.

As a school counselor, I once played a game called positive ball with my second grade class. The object of the game was to throw a ball from student to student. When a student threw the ball, they had to say something positive about the person they threw it to. This included something about their personality, characteristics, or even something simple like their clothes. The idea was to have a class who had been having difficulties getting along focus on and appreciate the good things about one another—to see each other as worthy and human.

One student threw the ball to a boy in the class. She said she really loved his shoes. The boy beamed at this statement and enthusiastically threw the ball to another, saying a kind statement. At the end of the game, I asked the students if anyone had told them something particularly special and meaningful. The boy raised his hand and, through tears, explained that the compliment he received about his shoes was so meaningful to him. His family didn't have a lot of money for new clothes, and he really, really loved these shoes, but since they were such a bright shade of blue, he was worried that other kids would make fun of them. He'd spent the whole day trying to evaluate whether other students had noticed or made fun of his shoes. His classmate sharing her positive opinion of his shoes made his entire day, brought him to tears, and caused these two students to connect. They played at recess and became friends in a way they hadn't before, as did many students in that class. Needless to say, arguments and problems in the class decreased for the rest of the year. I've had plenty of success playing positive ball with middle schoolers, undergraduate, and graduate students as well. We are all those children, so worried about appearances, so scared about being who we are, so willing to hear and embrace kindness in our lives.

We all hesitate to be kind to others, to listen and care and do the work to improve the world, especially when others let us down. The simple answer to how to handle the strife, division, and uncertainty of the world is to be kind. Kindness inspires the best in others. Kindness brings out the best in ourselves. Contemplation, discipline, and intentionality empower you to act in accordance with principles you truly believe, and to be in a place to help and inspire others. If you are not acting in a kind manner, if you are looking to use others for emotional validation, as an escape, or as a way to feel better about yourself, you are not being kind. You are setting yourself back, you are setting others back, and you are removed further from finding and being your best self.

I'm writing this section amid the COVID-19 outbreak. I've found that kindness truly inspires the best in others. My students, who have been forced into online learning, are dealing with many challenging life situations, including stressed finances, increased responsibilities as essential workers, and the loss of family members. I could be rigid in my requirements. Counselors must deal with this and be advocates for others, therefore the work requirements and the deadlines remain. However, in this context, understanding, kindness, and caring about my students as people have proven most effective. In fact, as I have relaxed some deadlines and requirements, I've seen students come forward with some of their best work of the semester, despite the harrowing circumstances. Why?

I always find that intrinsic motivation is the most powerful of all. These students appreciate kindness. They see I am investing in them as people and professionals, not just students who have to jump through hoops. This understanding, the shared kind words, the bonds, they lead to people wanting to do well. They provide people with the inspiration and energy to do their very best. My students have not taken advantage of my relaxed requirements—they recognize that I care and want the best for them, and in turn they strive to do the best they can in the moment out of appreciation and a desire to learn and grow into the best professionals they can be.

You can do this stuff every day, and trust me, it really does help how you feel about yourself, your purpose, and your life. You'll appreciate the little things, moments, and situations that much more. See the good in people and in the world, and you'll see the good in yourself too.

Do not use others. Be willing to hear them. Be willing to be wrong. Be willing to learn and grow. See the good and positives in people and situations. This doesn't mean ignore the bad; it means we don't primarily focus on it. Avoid absolutism—adjust for the situation and context. Be open, be mindful. Live every day—be present in the moment and then reflect on the moments in context. And finally, be kind, and love. Please, be kind and love, for your mind, body, and spirit and for that of others.

Be well, my friends. May you and your loved ones feel the happiness you deserve.